Profiles from the Kitchen

PROFILES FROM THE
Kitchen

WHAT GREAT COOKS HAVE TAUGHT US
ABOUT OURSELVES AND OUR FOOD

CHARLES A. BAKER-CLARK

THE UNIVERSITY PRESS OF KENTUCKY

Publication of this volume was made possible in part
by a grant from the National Endowment for the Humanities.

Scholarly publisher for the Commonwealth,
serving Bellarmine University, Berea College, Centre College of
Kentucky, Eastern Kentucky University, The Filson Historical Society,
Georgetown College, Kentucky Historical Society, Kentucky State
University, Morehead State University, Murray State University,
Northern Kentucky University, Transylvania University, University of
Kentucky, University of Louisville, and Western Kentucky University.
All rights reserved.

Editorial and Sales Offices: The University Press of Kentucky
663 South Limestone Street, Lexington, Kentucky 40508-4008
www.kentuckypress.com

10 09 08 07 06   5 4 3 2 1

Library of Congress Cataloging-in-Publication Data

Baker-Clark, Charles Allen.
 Profiles from the kitchen : what great cooks have taught us about ourselves
and our food / Charles A. Baker-Clark.
    p. cm.
 Includes bibliographical references and index.
 ISBN-13: 978-0-8131-2398-1 (hardcover : alk. paper)
 ISBN-10: 0-8131-2398-4 (hardcover : alk. paper)
 1. Cooks–United States–Biography. I. Title.
 TX649.A1B35 2006
 641.5092'273–dc22   2006001958

This book is printed on acid-free recycled paper meeting the requirements of the
American National Standard for Permanence in Paper for Printed Library Materials.

Manufactured in the United States of America.

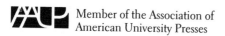 Member of the Association of
American University Presses

In loving memory of my father, Charlie,
known by friends and family as QU,
who bought me my first double-decker hamburger
at a place called Hamburger Heaven.

Contents

Acknowledgments

MY WORK HAS BEEN SHAPED by the footprints of many people who have walked into my life. Many of these have been teachers. Both the Rev. Emeric Janowski, a teacher at Immaculate Conception High School, and John Dirkx, my dissertation adviser, taught me the importance of believing in myself. It was an English composition instructor named Ridgely Pierson who helped me to appreciate the importance of my own voice.

There have been many other teachers in my life too numerous to mention. In particular, I want to thank the faculty of the Hospitality Education Department at Grand Rapids Community College, who shared their knowledge and passion for the culinary arts with me. I will never forget the cold January morning when I, a fortyish student, arrived nearly a week into classes to begin my culinary skills class and received a warm welcome from Chef James Muth, who invited me to enter his kitchen.

Other people in my life have been great role models. My grandfather, Ed, showed me the value of great stories and the joy associated with shared meals. Lester Zwick, a carpenter for more than eighty years, and whose sharp eye for detail and steady hands served him well in his finishing skills, demonstrated for me the importance of being a good craftsman. His daughter, Patti, has carried on this tradition of excellence through her work as a talented quilter.

My aunt, Marguerite Green, showed me how a teacher needs to both love her discipline and care about her students. A member of the Sacred Heart order of Catholic nuns, she was like a second mother to me. Both Marguerite and my mother, Jeanne, consistently demonstrated the importance of learning throughout life.

This book is based on an earlier project in which I examined the lives of Julia Child, James Beard, and Elizabeth David. I expanded the focus of the original project to include a number of other individuals and organizations that influence our relationship with food. In addition to the library research I conducted, I had an opportunity to meet with and interview Father Dominic Garramone, Rick Bayless, Susan Spicer, John T. Edge, John Thorne, Angus Campbell, and Mildred Council (Mama Dip). I am grateful to all of these individuals for taking the time to share their expertise with me.

Perhaps the most significant input for this book has been from my wife, Susan. She has encouraged me to experience all that life has to offer, and she has encouraged me to write. She has always fostered my growth as a person, and throughout this process she has been a constant source of advice and fresh ideas. She has helped me organize my work and has worked tirelessly as an editor. Thank you, Susan!

The Lost Connections to Our Food

It is disheartening to contemplate just how many people
there must be in the world for whom soup is something
that comes out of a can. Not that there aren't a few
laudable canned soups—the problem is that they are
few, expensive, and generally not quite up to what a good
soupmaker can turn out at home.
—Jonathan Bartlett, *The Peasant Gourmet*

WHEN I WAS A CHILD growing up in the west suburbs of Chicago, my parents took me and my younger siblings to a small resort
town in Michigan nearly every summer. Mom and all of us children
would stay in my grandmother's cottage and dad would join us for
weekends. Summer food at the cottage was simple but fun to prepare. We learned to cook hot dogs over an open fire and to make ed-
ible pizzas from boxed mixes that cost less than fifty cents. In a style
similar to childhood time spent by food essayist John Thorne on the
coast of Maine, we picked berries in season. We ate nature's bounty
by the bowlful, with cream or sprinkled over homemade ice cream
produced with a hand-operated churn. Mom baked pies and made
muffins and pancakes that ran purple with the juice of blueberries.

For decades a worn copy of *The Joy of Cooking* stood watch in the
small cottage kitchen. This book charted many a culinary adventure

beyond the realm of fried chicken and waffles. Cooking at the cottage became a part of our summer life — a form of entertainment. In fact, one of my aunts refused to set foot in the cottage, exclaiming that when she went on vacation she wanted to get away from cooking and cleaning. We had a ball.

When we were staying at the cottage, we rarely dined out. There were no fast-food outlets, just a few locally owned restaurants and bars and a nice place where we purchased pizza. One of these was a small seasonal sandwich stand that sold, among other items, Bogey dogs and Bogey burgers. In particular, I recall being fascinated by the notion of a Bogey dog. Humphrey Bogart was one of my idols, and I could imagine myself dressed in a white dinner jacket ordering a pair of Bogey dogs. "You made 'em for her. You can make 'em for me. Make 'em, Sam. Gimme two Bogey dogs." My parents were skeptical about the relative merit of Bogey dogs, especially since they cost approximately $1.75 apiece. Mom and dad were about halfway through producing nine offspring and did not have the discretionary income to pay that much for their son's food fantasies. My father would say, "If you want hot dogs, we can make them for you. I'm not buying you a hot dog at that ridiculous price. Case closed."

A few years later, I found myself back at the cottage. I was an adolescent and had a few dollars of my own that were burning a hole in my pocket. One afternoon I walked down to the waterfront and stepped up to the counter of that same sandwich stand. I told the man working there that I wanted two Bogey dogs and forked over nearly four dollars. This was a substantial investment considering the fact that the transaction occurred a number of years before McDonald's rolled out their Big Mac sandwich priced at slightly more than fifty cents each.

When he handed me my purchase, I was stunned and felt betrayed. "These are just hot dogs!" I said. "That's right," he replied. "But what makes them Bogey dogs?" He sneered at me. "I call them Bogey dogs because I feel like calling them Bogey dogs."

If we fast-forward from this incident in the sixties to the present, we can readily spot similar artifacts in contemporary culture. Sometimes it seems as though all of the food manufacturers and chain-restaurant operators want us to believe they are providing the biggest, newest, and best taste sensation we have ever experienced. Is it possible that they are also selling us Bogey dogs?

This condition is regrettable, especially since food forms such an integral part of our lives. After all, our health depends on an adequate supply of nutrients. However, food and cooking are also integrally intertwined with our identities. For example, M. F. K. Fisher (1990) describes food as being intertwined with security and love. Thelma Barer-Stein (1999), who writes about the influence of ethnic heritage on the foods we eat, echoes this sentiment: "There is no cultural group and no individual for whom at least one specific food—the memory, taste or smell of which—does not evoke a pang of loving nostalgia" (14). Sidney Saylor Farr (1983) also writes about people formerly from Appalachia who, when asked about what they miss the most about their region, mention food—particular cornbread and soup beans—and the conversations held around the kitchen table. These writers reveal only a small aspect of the complex relationship between people and their food. Perhaps food is a part of our lives that we must continually rediscover. What could be a more satisfying pastime?

In their seminal book on the anthropology of eating, Farb and Armelagos (1982) also provide interesting examples of the cultural importance of food and eating. They refer to the connection between eating and spiritual experiences and celebrations that occur in many different cultures. An example of this from our culture is found in New Orleans prior to Lent. At that time of year it is traditional to serve collops (eggs fried on top of bacon) on the Monday before Ash Wednesday (Wolf 1996). This dish is identified with the day, known as Collop Monday, because many people traditionally give up eggs and bacon during Lent. Thus, the different foods we eat and how they are prepared provide information not only about who we are as individuals but also about the nature of our culture.

Our culture in the United States is an amalgam of the contributions of many different immigrant groups combined with a variety of indigenous peoples. We are Neapolitan, Huguenot, Acadian, Quaker, Bantu, Cantonese, Sri Lankan, and Iroquois. Our food pathways, in particular, reflect this rich and interesting set of traditions. Chef Stephan Pyles (1993) provides a striking example of the cultural complexity of food in this country when he points to at least thirty-two different ethnic influences affecting the cooking of the people of Texas.

However, the rich texture provided by our diverse ethnic, familial, and regional backgrounds is at risk of being lost. We can see examples of this in what Carlo Petrini (2001) refers to as the steamrolling of culture. For example, ask the average American about Italian food and the conversation will invariably focus on pizza, lasagna, spaghetti, and fettuccine Alfredo. This disintegrates further into pizza burgers, Italian subs, and canned spaghetti. Moreover, the meals offered in Italian American restaurants all too often feature portions of epic size and foods covered with gobs of melted factory cheese. Lost in the conversation are rice dishes such as risotto Milanese, prosciutto crudo, pastas that are not drowned in tomato or cream sauces, and the styles of dining in Italy that differ markedly from the eat-and-run meals consumed in U.S. homes and restaurants. Don't ask Kyle, your server at the nearest outlet of an Italian-style chain restaurant, about anything genuinely Italian. He probably does not know very much beyond what he may have been spoon-fed by the corporation that owns the restaurant. He is probably most interested in serving your food pronto, collecting his tip, and getting you out the door so he can seat the next round of customers. You can expect the same type of service and lack of cultural knowledge whether you visit their outlets in Cleveland, Miami, or San Francisco.

In addition to the homogenization of food and dining experiences, cooking and eating have regrettably become virtual assembly-line activities that we manage to squeeze rather easily into our busy daily routines. We can see evidence of this in the vacant stares of people waiting in line at drive-up lanes of fast-food outlets and those who eat while driving. Who has the time to cook? We are told by advertisers that we have better things to do, such as earn more money and be compliant and passive consumers. Who has the time these days to sit down and enjoy a quiet meal with family or friends? Perhaps this is a matter of progress. If so, how long will it be before we, in the words of Sidney Mintz (1996), will be force-fed semidigested nutrients by food manufacturers? It should come as no surprise, therefore, that Sally Tisdale (2000) remarked that in the United States there is now no one to teach the craft of cooking—and no one to learn it.

In the United States our relationship with food has evolved considerably over the past 150 years. Over the past century, traditional food production and preparation methods have changed dramatically. The technological advances of the nineteenth and twentieth centuries, together with improvements in the transportation system, have combined to produce a remarkably efficient production and distribution network for agricultural products. Cooking methods have also evolved dramatically as a result of technological improvements. The simplification of cooking procedures and food products has become an increasingly popular theme throughout the twentieth century. The food industry developed mass-marketing strategies as huge corporations such as Nabisco and Heinz strove to profit from the nation's expanding appetite. Food producers also developed products such as cake mixes and frozen dinners that simplified cooking procedures for people who were too busy to cook. Cooking was soon being classified alongside similar household chores as "drudgery."

While food producers were creating innovative products, an entire industry of "labor-saving" kitchen appliances such as the blender and the food processor was emerging. In addition to promoting efficiency, advertisements for these devices also touted their cutting-edge modernity. A housewife without a mixer or other equally "essential" appliances ran the risk of appearing old-fashioned to her friends and family. It is perhaps this indiscriminate acquisition of kitchen appliances and gadgets that prompted Julia Child to remark: "In department stores, so much kitchen equipment is bought indiscriminately by people who just come in for men's underwear" (Simpson 1988).

I was born into this era, when science and technology were viewed as having the capacity to solve all our problems. For example, it was during this period that the microwave oven was developed and became popular. I can still vividly recall having breakfast at a friend's home and listening to his father extol the wonders of the microwave-prepared bacon we were eating. We thought that technology would soon be capable of developing machines that, as in Jane Jetson's world, could produce entire meals from pills. Life would be effortless and nearly perfect.

In the middle of this march toward utopia, a representative of a milkshake machine manufacturer named Ray Kroc traveled to California in order to meet the McDonald brothers, owners of a highly successful drive-in restaurant. This encounter helped spur the rapid development and proliferation of an entirely new segment of the foodservice industry, namely, fast food.

One factor that made the McDonald brothers' restaurant so successful was their application of assembly-line production principles to food preparation. Armed with a simple menu, the restaurant could be staffed with relatively inexperienced and consequently cheaper labor. In this situation, one cook would fry preportioned hamburgers on a flat-top grill while another would place the burgers on buns and add condiments, while yet another would wrap and bag the finished products to be passed "out the window" to customers.

Other franchisors and restaurant chains followed suit. Technological advances and management principles, such as "just in time purchasing," have made the process even more efficient. This has been complemented by different service options, such as drive-through window service and self-service beverage dispensers.

These advances, moreover, were mirrored by the creation of efficient, structured procedures to be followed by customers, who obediently line up at counters to order their meals based on a preassigned number. Customers' orders are entered into a point-of-sale system that typically features pictures of food items to simplify the process and reduce the chance of error. When orders are complete, customers tote their food to tables, dispense their own beverages, devour the food in short order, and bus their own tables, all of this being accomplished with maximum efficiency. After all, don't we have better things to do with our valuable time?

Developments in the foodservice industry reflect more than a shift in food production, marketing strategies, and eating preferences. They have also heralded dramatic changes in American lifestyles, including the exodus from cities to suburbia and an increased reliance on the automobile as a form of transportation. When family incomes began to be based on two or more wage earners, efficient food preparation became paramount. This situation was compounded with an increase in the average number of hours worked per week. As children began to take on more commitments such as part-time employment, meals became abbreviated.

As the demand for convenience food and "convenient eating" became more acute, the foodservice industry responded with an increasing array of convenience food and food-preparation technology. TV dinners, microwaveable meals, instant rice, and canned foods pandered to American tastes, with shoppers avoiding the aisles offering fresh produce in favor of those with boxed and frozen products.

As the baby-boom generation became ever more independent and affluent, the foodservice industry also adapted to their tastes and spending habits. Fast-food outlets were augmented by chain restaurants offering specialized menus such as quasi-authentic ethnic foods and alcoholic beverages. Typically these restaurants were based on a casual theme that appealed to a generation whose standard uniform for virtually all occasions consisted of blue jeans and ball caps. An example of this phenomenon has been the proliferation of Mexican-style restaurants offering foods such as refried beans laced with lard and topped with processed melted cheese and sour cream. What do dishes such as these have to do with the cuisine of Mexico?

In the same decade that saw the expansion of chain restaurants, the popularity of gourmet cooking increased exponentially. Cookware and department stores offered expanded lines of cookware, cutlery, and a vast array of gadgets. Many of these same retailers began offering cooking demonstrations as well as cooking classes. To be considered a "gourmet cook" became a mark of social success. Unfortunately, all too often the most powerful lesson associated with gourmet cooking has been an appreciation for the cost of ingredients, gadgets, and lessons. For example, a set of top-quality kitchen knives can go for as much as six hundred dollars, while trend-setting cookware can cost one hundred dollars or more per pan. One wonders how much the quality of cooking has increased as a result of these inflated price tags. Fried potatoes cut with an expensive French knife and sautéed in an expensive pan do not necessarily turn out tastier than those made by your grandmother, whose primary cooking utensils consisted of a few battered pans and one or two knives—or in John Thorne's reliable cast iron skillet.

Velma (Grandma) Hutchings, with her special fork and a few pans, would have scoffed at the mention of gourmet cooking. Cooking was simply an important component of her life. After all, Grandma had once cooked for threshers with boundless appetites, and she was more than willing to relieve them of some of their spending money in a few hands of cards after dinner.

Grandma Hutchings would have felt lost in a world of programmable coffeemakers and bread machines. Perhaps this older-generation cook represents a time long past from this modernized and highly technical world. However, Velma possessed valuable knowledge derived from her extended family as well as other personal sources of information. The power of this form of knowledge is adroitly illustrated by Aurora Levins Morales (1997): "When I lift the lid from that big black pot, my kitchen fills with the hands of women who came before me, washing rice, washing beans" (296). We must begin to reclaim this knowledge about both cooking and eating. The quality of our lives partially depends on it.

In general, the development of food production in the United States has heralded a loss of craft knowledge. It has also created an increase in costs associated with cooking good food. The rice industry illustrates both problems. Cooking rice from scratch has never been a daunting task. Depending on the desired result, rice cookery has typically involved combining water, rice, and a little salt. The mixture is then simmered in a covered pan for approximately twenty minutes, fluffed with a fork, and served. Although this process hardly demands a high degree of skill, the rice industry now provides par-cooked rice as well as minute rice. For those who find the measurement of water to be an insurmountable task, there is also boil-in-a-bag rice and microwaveable rice. The more adventurous can also purchase rice combinations offering an exotic array of flavors such as curry, Creole, and risotto. We are repeatedly told that we have better things to do than to prepare our own food, that our lives are too busy. We are not, however, reminded that we have become a society of obese couch potatoes as a result of consuming overly processed foods containing high levels of fat, salt, and sugar.

The preparation options for rice also illustrate the increase in cost associated with convenience. Consider the difference between purchasing long grain rice in bulk—say, five pounds or more—as opposed to purchasing microwaveable rice in small quantities. The cost to society at large is even greater when we consider the loss of knowledge associated with the simple act of preparing rice from scratch. One must also consider the problem of waste products associated with convenience foods such as microwaveable rice. Even if we ignore the waste associated with their production, these products represent a major source of waste. They are typically produced in boxes with flavor packets included. The individual boxes are packed in cartons for shipping. Think of the quantities of paper and cardboard that end up in landfills as a result of millions of these packaged convenience products!

Our relationship to food and its preparation has been greatly influenced by the individuals described in this book. We owe an enormous debt to them, as well to the multitude of professionals who are not mentioned. We have a lot to learn from the lives of these subjects. Paul and Julia Child have accomplished far more than the simplification of French cooking. Indeed, they have also served as exemplars of teaching and learning in adulthood. Scottish chef and culinary educator Angus Campbell exemplifies the role of passion in teaching his subject. He embodies what A. J. Liebling (1959) has referred to as the virtue of a hearty appetite for many different foods. James Beard has taught us about food while simultaneously weaving elements of his childhood and other stories into his lessons. Michael Ruhlman has taught us about what it takes to truly learn a craft.

John T. Edge, John Thorne, and Dennis Getto have also written passionately about good food. John T. Edge writes about interesting places where one can discover both food and local traditions while recounting stories of the people associated with these places. John Thorne also extols the virtues of cooking and eating simply. Dennis Getto, a restaurant critic in Milwaukee, writes about great places to eat, not limiting his research to upscale eateries by also providing information on where to find a good hot dog or where to find fried fish during the Lenten season. Finally, Father Dominic Garramone writes about his passion for bread and its close connection to our spiritual well-being.

Many of these individuals have also written extensively about the cultures where interesting foods can be found. Elizabeth David, for example, has written about the genius that shines from the pans of the Mediterranean. Rick Bayless continues to rediscover Mexico's rich culinary heritage and its complex cuisines.

Still others encourage us to examine aspects of food that we may have overlooked. Eugene Walter teases us as he describes interesting anecdotes associated with food and cookery. M. F. K. Fisher writes about the quirkiness and sensuality of food, while John T. Edge writes passionately about a variety of food-related topics, including the role of food in a just and civil society. The latter concept is also emphasized by the Slow Food movement in stressing such important issues as regional identity and traceability of the foods we consume.

Finally, we recognize the embodiment of a great crafts person in Susan Spicer, who modestly describes herself as "a working chef." Susan's pursuit of her craft has set her apart from other "celebrity chefs" who may be all the rage today.

Too many of these individuals have passed on. Elizabeth David, M. F. K. Fisher, Julia Child's coauthor and close friend Simone Beck, and Paul Child all died within a few months of each other. And finally, we have lost our favorite cook, namely, Julia Child. However, thanks to their legacies we can discover and rediscover many important lessons about cooking and dining.

This education in both taste and craft has evolved over several generations and continues to develop as I write. These individuals have shared insights with us concerning their personal relationship with food and have taught us numerous lessons about food, culture, and the great craft of cooking. Nevertheless, the most powerful lessons in these areas are those that we create for ourselves—and for others. I invite you to join us in the kitchen and at the table.

References

Barer-Stein, T. 1999. *You Eat What You Are: People, Culture and Food Traditions.* Buffalo, N.Y.: Firefly Books.

Bartlett, J. 1975. *The Peasant Gourmet.* New York: Macmillan.

Farb, P., and G. Armelagos. 1982. *Consuming Passions: The Anthropology of Eating.* Boston, Mass.: Houghton Mifflin.

Farr, S. S. 1983. *More Than Moonshine: Appalachian Recipes and Recollections.* Pittsburgh, Pa: University of Pittsburgh Press.

Fisher, M. F. K. 1990. *The Art of Eating.* New York: John Wiley.

Levins Morales, A. 1997. Kitchens. In *Through the Kitchen Window: Women Explore the Intimate Meanings of Food and Cooking,* ed. A. Voski Avakian, 296–98. Boston, Mass.: Beacon Press.

Liebling, A. J. 1959. *Between Meals: An Appetite for Paris.* New York: Simon and Schuster.

Mintz, S. 1996. *Tasting Food, Tasting Freedom: Excursions into Eating, Culture and the Past*. Boston, Mass.: Beacon Press.

Petrini, C. 2001. *Slow Food: The Case for Taste*. New York: Columbia University Press.

Pyles, S. 1993. *New Texas Cuisine*. New York: Doubleday.

Simpson, J. 1988. *Simpson's Contemporary Quotations: The Most Notable Quotes Since 1950*. Boston, Mass.: Houghton Mifflin. Accessed June 21, 2004, at http://www.bartleby.com/63/85/6385.html.

Tisdale, S. 2000. *The Best Thing I Ever Tasted: The Secret of Food*. New York: Riverhead Books.

Wolf, B. 1996. *Gatherings and Celebrations: History, Folklore, Rituals and Recipes for the Occasions That Bring People Together*. New York: Doubleday.

James Beard

The Dean of American Cookery

When you cook, you never stop learning.
—James Beard, *James Beard's Theory
and Practice of Good Cooking*

JAMES ANDREWS BEARD was born in Portland, Oregon, in 1903. The only child of Mary Elizabeth and John Beard, he grew up in a home where good food and cooking were paramount. The locale in which the Beards lived was a vibrant, new community situated in the Willamette Valley, a region later described as a "Garden of Eden" because of its rich natural resources and people (Oregon Historical Society 2004). During this period Portland experienced rapid expansion as many Americans and Europeans made the city their home.

Life in Portland at the beginning of the twentieth century was a stimulating environment, and it had a significant impact on young Beard. Some of the most interesting descriptions of Portland at that time come from his own writing. In fact, he frequently interspersed his writing about food and cooking with fond memories of his childhood. For example, Beard described the city as "rich with magnificent houses" and possessing a "raw vitality." Among these memories, his depiction of Portland as a city abounding with good food found in hotels, restaurants, and markets stands out.

In Portland Mary Beard owned and managed a small hotel, the Gladstone. Much of her work was centered on the management of the kitchen. (She subsequently sold the Gladstone and moved the family into a home on Salmon Street, where she took in boarders while continuing to maintain a busy kitchen.) It was not unusual for her to ride her bicycle nearly five miles to the market every day to conduct her shopping. The image of Mary Beard investing so much energy in grocery shopping is reminiscent of Madame Barette's dedicated shopping for her family's food at the great marketplace of Les Halles (David 1980) and her subsequent influence on British food writer Elizabeth David.

Much of the food available in the Portland area could be purchased in the city's great public marketplace. For example, the variety of regional available fish was staggering, including cod, halibut, smelt, steelhead, sturgeon, and salmon.

As a child, James Beard learned about food in the same way Julia Child and Elizabeth David did when they visited French marketplaces. When it came to shopping at the marketplace, Mary set a powerful example for her son, who often accompanied her. Her forays into the market were frequent and often notorious. Mary's standards for food were legendary, as illustrated by the following story related by Beard: "I particularly remember one very early visit to the market in the company of my nursemaid. We had just been to the doctor's and on the way back stopped to buy a few things for my mother. When they were wrapped and handed to the maid, she said quietly, 'Please charge them to Mrs. Beard.' The clerk blanched and said, 'For God's sake, give me that package. If I sent that to *her*, she'd kill me!'" (Beard 1992, 49).

It was in the marketplace, as well as in his home, that James learned to appreciate a broad range of foods. Beard later described his exposure to new foods encountered in the marketplace: "One could even find morels in the market. I remember the first time I saw them. I was quite shocked by their appearance. To me they resembled dried-up brains (they still do) and I couldn't imagine what they were" (49). For the young James Beard eating became an adventure that persisted throughout life.

Regrettably, it is difficult to imagine how eating in contemporary America could be very adventuresome when all too many menus offer a relatively safe and limited bill of fare to customers. Is it still possible for today's parents to create excitement in cooking and eating in the family kitchen without resorting to the familiar convenience foods?

James Beard's early experiences with interesting foods and his contact with passionate cooks influenced his later teaching and writing. For example, in his writing Beard insisted that cooks need to remain open to new products and experiences. He frequently encouraged beginning cooks to learn through the development of taste. He also emphasized the need for cooks to be practical and to use products that were locally produced, seasonally fresh, and readily available. This sentiment has become a mantra for chefs across the country.

It is hardly surprising that James developed his preference for good, fresh foods from his mother. However, Mary's purchases also invariably involved the development of close friendships with many vendors. In his autobiography James discussed his mother's relationship with a local vegetable purveyor named Delfino. This purveyor grew and sold sweet basil. From him Mary learned how to use basil to make pesto and other dishes. Delfino would frequently visit the Beard home, being as much a friend to the family as he was a supplier of good food.

These early experiences instilled in Beard both an appreciation for the importance of purchasing good food and the need to form positive social relationships with vendors and others in the marketplace. In fact, Beard later commented: "No market is too small to captivate me. In each I discover new foods, new challenges" (59). The fact that consumers can interact with producers of their food is a factor that animates the farmers' markets in many communities and also explains why they are supported by organizations such as the Greater Grand Rapids Food Systems Council.

The Floyd Boulevard Local Foods Market

Promoting Local Foods and Conviviality

The farmers' market is part general store and part church social.
I talk to strangers whom I would never have met were it
not for our common love of fresh food.
—M. Wisdom, "Pressing the Fresh"

It was 8 A.M. on a Saturday in May 2004. Father Marvin Boes, director of the Diocesan Peace and Justice Commission of the Catholic Diocese of Sioux City, Iowa, rang a farmyard bell to signal the opening of a new kind of farmers' market (Bedford 2004). This market promotes only local foods produced in natural and humane environments. A project of the organization Sustainable Foods for Siouxland, this farmers' market strives to maintain a "humane and sustainable local food supply for the region" (Rosman 2004). While James Beard did not strongly support the use of organic foods, he certainly would have been interested in the struggle of this young marketplace to become an integral part of its local culture.

In other communities similar forces are beginning to emphasize the need to promote locally produced foods. For example, in Vermont the Farmers' Diner features pictures of local food producers who have supplied ingredients for the menu (Halweil 2003). On the West Coast Alice Waters promotes the importance of teaching children about where their foods originate by incorporating food into the K–12 school curriculum (McManus 2004).

The movement favoring a closer connection between consumers and small-scale food producers represents a form of rebellion against what Father Marvin Boes calls a factory farming system (Lefebvre 2002). One way farmers' markets such as the Floyd Boulevard Local Foods Market militate against this "factory system" is by promoting local food producers (Bedford 2004; Freiburger 2004). It should come as no surprise that the Floyd Boulevard market's motto that includes words such as healthy, humane, and homegrown (Freiburger 2004).

The Floyd Boulevard market specifies how foods are to be produced and animals sold are to be raised. It is also important to consider what else might draw consumers to its venue. There are social and emotional factors associated with these markets that cannot be replicated in giant superstores. There is a sense of community shared by people who participate in farmers' markets like the Floyd Boulevard market.

Just as Slow Food's great event, Terre Madre, drew thousands of food producers from around the world to create "food communities," markets such as the one located on Floyd Boulevard represent opportunities to form health communities on a smaller scale. These markets are cropping up in villages and neighborhoods across the United States. If this is a form of rebellion, it certainly is a flavorful one.

The importance of connections with other people through cooking and eating consequently becomes evident as an important thread throughout Beard's life, as well as that of other individuals described in this book. Unfortunately, this does not often appear in the literature dedicated to teaching and learning about cooking and is found even less frequently in the arena of cookbooks. It also does not resonate with the current "search and destroy" shopping that can be observed every day in the sterile atmosphere of today's supermarkets.

James Beard's family was highly active in Portland's social life and their home was the venue for various events. These gatherings were frequently highlighted by rich and elaborate meals prepared in their home by Mary Elizabeth Beard and the family cook, Jue-Let "Let." James later described the family kitchen as a social hub for the neighborhood. It was in this house that family and friends gathered for holiday meals that required days of preparation

James Beard's early cooking skills arose, in part, from his exposure to the passion and dedication of family members. Mary Beard demonstrated this when she painstakingly grilled food at the beach. She would cook fish or steak over glowing coals, brushing the flesh with bacon fat or butter and tending the food carefully until it was grilled to perfection. Beard later drew upon these early experiences when he wrote and taught about the art of grilling.

In addition to his mother's influence, James Beard was strongly affected by the family cook, Let, as well as his father's cooking. A case in point was John Beard's careful preparation of Sunday breakfast. He would handslice bacon and cook it over low heat until it was done. He would then use the hot rendered fat to cook chicken. The last stage of his ritual was the creation of milk gravy.

James Beard used phrases such as "work of art" to describe the cookery of his parents and Let. The care that John Beard applied to his work reveals the Beard family's recognition that the process of cooking was as important to its members as the final products that were consumed. This was, above all, a family that valued cooking as a special activity and not just a chore to be dispensed with as quickly and efficiently as possible. The craft of cooking thus became a symbol of the Beard family's identity, just as it was for the grandparents of Eugene Walter.

From the subtle rhythms of the Beard household James developed a deep and abiding appreciation for food and cooking, as well as a complex set of culinary skills. His childhood explorations of food and cooking occurred under many different circumstances both inside and outside the kitchen. As a toddler, he explored his mother's kitchen and tasted nearly everything. He also watched Mary and Let cook. The young James also spent a considerable amount of time at the beach. The family often held cookouts there and James would frequently hunt razor clams for his mother to sauté. Later in childhood James taught other children the art of capturing those same clams, which burrow rapidly in the wet sand to escape one's reach.

The techniques James learned from different family members did not have to be complicated in order to prove useful. Beard has suggested that much of the craft of cooking may be built upon a mastery of simple techniques, such as the following: "Let had been taught to soak the currants well before folding them into the dough [for currant bread]. What a flavor this gave, and how it puzzled many of the friends who came to tea and tried to uncover this simple secret" (36). Perhaps the greatest "secret" Beard and other cooks have learned is that many useful cooking skills are quite simple. This is also reflected in Julia Child's insistence that great cooking does not have to be based on the creation of complicated gastronomic masterpieces but rather on the sensible use of good, fresh foods.

As James Beard continued to mature, he became increasingly interested in the theater and opera. He participated in high school and community theater productions. After graduating from high school, he entered Reed College, where he ended his formal education in less than a year. Mary offered to subsidize his voice training for an operatic career. Both agreed that James needed to get out of Portland and study in Europe under the tutelage of a professional voice coach.

Beard subsequently embarked on the *Highland Heather*, a freighter bound for England, in pursuit of an operatic career. It was 1922, and the trip proved memorable. James's first encounter with an international marketplace occurred when the ship docked at the island of Saint Thomas.

In London Beard trained as an opera singer under the direction of Gaetano "Tano" Loria, a voice coach who had once worked with Caruso. Perhaps the most significant culinary education during this stage of his life was Beard's exposure to the cosmopolitan atmosphere of London and Paris and their food markets. He dined out as often as his budget would permit, frequently as the guest of Gaetano and his wife, who would often dine in the company of affluent friends. They also took him out to the countryside in order to harvest wild greens for salads (Jones 1990). Cooking and eating with friends became an important aspect of Beard's life, as it is with many people who are skilled cooks. This socialization process is not a way to parade a cook's skills but rather a wonderful means of teaching and learning about food.

While living in London and on visits to Paris, Beard regularly frequented the great marketplaces of Covent Garden and Les Halles.

Concerning Covent Garden, in addition to commenting on the surprising variety of available products, Beard also talked about how he learned by simply observing the way business was conducted at the market. In a similar vein, Beard described the Paris marketplace of Les Halles, which he described as a nexus of ideas regarding cooking: "I have had the experience of going to market with a number of restaurateurs and have observed them making a first round to collect ideas while they kept close watch that no one else got something he wanted at a lower price" (Beard 1992, 95). Once again Beard acknowledged the importance of the culture of the marketplace and how people seemed to benefit from their relationships involving food and cooking. He also expressed an interest in the wide assortment of products available, commenting on the great range in quality of particular products. This was true not only of vegetables and fruits but of fish, fowl, game, and meat as well. We can see how these experiences deepened Beard's knowledge of different foods.

Cooking and entertaining became a means for James of stretching his limited budget. While his mother did provide him with a stipend, it was just enough to support a bohemian lifestyle and not the more refined one he preferred (Clark 1996). It is probable that James cooked many meals for himself and his friends, as he did in later years. This skill helped him through other financially challenging times.

James Beard returned to the United States in 1924 upon the insistence of his mother, who was unwilling to provide additional funds for him to remain in Europe. Instead of returning to Portland, Beard traveled from England to New York City. He attempted to obtain work as an actor and subsequently returned to Portland after failing to find viable employment. In Portland he secured a position with a theater company. He also worked for a radio broadcasting company. In 1927 Beard traveled to Hollywood and was able to land minor parts in several films, including DeMille's *King of Kings* (Clark 1996).

After several years of failed attempts to find steady employment in the film industry, Beard returned first to Seattle, where he stayed until 1931, and then moved back to Portland, where he lived with his parents. He again found steady work as a radio performer and landed major roles in several plays. Throughout this stage of Beard's life he continued to develop his cooking skills and was able to use them to meet people and form social alliances. A case in point is when Beard invited Cecil B. DeMille and his family and cooked the meal. It was also at this time that Beard was able to earn some extra income by teaching others how to cook. In Portland he made the acquaintance of Agnes Crowther, an interior designer. Shortly thereafter, James began organizing cooking lessons for her clients.

In 1937 James Beard returned to New York in a final attempt to establish himself as an actor. He also tried to find work backstage in costume and set design. Although Beard experienced constant frustration in this area, his cooking skills continued to develop. On many occasions he was able to utilize these skills to help support himself. His friends would often pay for the ingredients and Beard would "earn" a meal through his cooking.

It was through Beard's expanding social contacts that he was able to make the acquaintance of Bill Rhode and his sister, Irma (Beard 1992; Clark 1996; Jones 1990). Together the three of them developed a catering business called Hors d'Oeuvres, Inc. This business was designed to provide food for the numerous cocktail parties that occurred nightly in Manhattan. The business was an immediate success and was given a favorable review by Lucius Beebe in the *New York Times* (Jones 1990).

Shortly after Hors d'Oeuvres, Inc., opened for business, James Beard was engaged in food preparation on a full-time basis. The popularity of Hors d' Oeuvres, Inc., resulted in new and important connections for Beard. One such connection developed from a telephone call he received from Jeanne Owen, a prominent fixture of the New York food scene. Beard would later comment that Owen was instrumental in helping him refine his culinary skills. She also assisted in furthering Beard's career through her numerous connections in the food world.

The influence of Jeanne Owen on James Beard was substantial. In a way, Owen replaced Beard's mother as his mentor following Mary Beard's death in 1940. She and James visited many restaurants together in a way similar to that in which James had accompanied Mary and John when they dined out. However, Owen's teaching of more formal cooking theory and skills extended the knowledge James had gained from his mother, which was later reflected in his own teaching.

It was Beard's connection to Jeanne Owen that facilitated the publication of his first book, *Hors d'Oeuvres and Canapés* (1940). This book has experienced a lasting following and remains in print today. In 1942 Beard published *Cook It Outdoors*. This was followed in 1944 by *Fowl & Game Cookery*.

During World War II Beard continued to expand his knowledge of food and cooking. He worked as a roving manager of clubs for sailors in the American Merchant Marine. In this capacity Beard had to hire cooking staff and design menus. At times his work involved training staff, which expanded his education. Since most of these clubs were located overseas, his position provided him with an opportunity to learn about different cultures and cooking techniques.

After the war, Beard had an opportunity to audition for a role on a television program that was being broadcast in New York City. His acting and radio experience provided him with the requisite skills for anchoring a regular cooking segment on a program called *For You and Yours*. Beard's segment was so popular that NBC designed a show for him called *Elsie Presents James Beard in "I Love to Eat!"* This show ran from August 1946 through May 1947 but was cancelled due to lack of sponsorship.

James Beard's popularity continued to grow throughout the fifties. In addition to publishing more books, he began to write columns for various periodicals, including *McCall's*, *Ladies' Home Journal*, and *House & Garden*. Beard's expertise in cooking was not limited to writing for women's magazines. His understanding of outdoor and game cookery also made him a popular writer for such men's magazines as *Argosy*.

During this period James Beard became intensely involved in teaching cookery. A significant way to learn is to engage in the practice of teaching, and Beard's potential as an effective teacher of the culinary arts became increasingly apparent. In fact, the food historian Betty Fussell (1983) has written that toward the end of his life Beard had taught cooking to professionals and amateurs for nearly thirty years. If we include his work with Agnes Crowther in Portland, Beard's experience in teaching the craft was even greater. Significantly, Fussell recognized that Beard's cooking *and* teaching had made him a "genuine folk hero" (80). Although the past century produced many heroes associated with cooking, it is difficult to conjure up many names of individuals who taught cooking with the skill and depth of understanding that one associates with the name of James Beard.

Beard founded his cooking school in 1955 in partnership with André Surmain. By 1957 Beard and Surmain had parted ways and the school, renamed the James Beard Cooking School (Clark 1996), was located in Beard's town house in New York City. For decades small groups of students attended Beard's lectures and hands-on demonstrations (Skow 1966). The students who took classes with James Beard became his devoted followers, with many enrolling year after year. This was the result of more than Beard's expertise in the kitchen. He radiated passion for his subject and a devotion to those who wanted to learn the craft. Beard's summary of his approach to cooking reveals his feelings for the entire process: "In my twenty-five years of teaching I have tried to make people realize that cooking is primarily fun and the more they know about what they are doing, the more fun it is. I love having them ask questions because that's the only way they are going to understand a term or technique. When I spot a student who is hungry to know all the whys and hows and wherefores, I try to encourage his or her inquisitiveness, knowing that this is the first sign of a creative cook" (Beard 1992, xi).

In her introduction to *James Beard's Theory & Practice of Good Cooking (1977)*, Barbara Kafka, who also taught with Beard on various occasions, discusses Beard's approach to teaching how to cook and concludes: "Teaching was what Jim loved best" (ix). She also points to Beard's capacity to establish a rapport with students, as well as his passion, knowledge, and the orderliness of his thinking as contributing to the learning that occurred in his kitchen. It is likely that Beard derived a certain percentage of this organization of culinary knowledge from his relationship with Jeanne Owen. Beard's ability to establish rapport and organize information for students must also have stimulated the learning atmosphere in his kitchen.

As Beard developed his skills as a cook and teacher, he began to emphasize the emotional aspect of learning to cook. In various interviews and articles Beard stressed the need to think of cooking as a fun activity. In fact, in one interview (Skow 1966) he challenged the notion that cooking is toilsome: "If you're convinced that cooking is a drudgery, you're never going to be any good at it, and you might as well warm up something frozen" (30). In her introductory note to *James Beard's Theory & Practice of Good Cooking*, Julia Child stated that Beard was "an endearing and always lively teacher, he loved people, loved his work, loved gossip, loved to eat, loved a good time" (vi). This statement echoes Beard's remark that he wanted to convey the notion that cooking is enjoyable.

Beard also emphasized the adventurous nature of cooking. In a *People* magazine interview (Stewart 1981) Beard indicated that a sense of adventure meant being willing to try unfamiliar ingredients: "If I have a class and prepare certain foods, such as kidneys and tripe, people will say, 'Oh, no, I can't eat it.' That was probably instilled in them in childhood, just as some people won't touch calf's liver or beef tongue because of prejudice" (64). But Beard also pointed to the importance of experimenting with new ideas. This is exemplified in an article (1964) Beard wrote about liqueurs: "In the kitchen, try new tricks with liqueurs. Baste pork with an orange liqueur or crêpes with a raspberry liqueur" (218). Surely Beard's learning up to this point reflected the Chinese proverb that one must possess an adventurous spirit in order to eat well.

Much of the learning associated with James Beard's teaching was experiential. For example, he frequently taught lessons that involved the use of the senses. Beard wanted learners to develop a discriminating sense of taste as he had. In an interview published in *House & Garden* magazine (Erwitt 1981), Beard discussed the need for students to develop a sense of taste: "Barbara Kafka and I give classes on taste and the results are fascinating. Students sniff and taste ingredients raw, then compare flavors as ingredients are cooked using different methods. The new knowledge makes them more sensitive, better cooks" (151). In another article (Fussell 1983) Beard is quoted telling cooks to be bold and taste things for themselves: "Taste things half done, done and overdone" (80). Here is evidence of the interaction between sensory knowledge and trial and error.

Another experiential method utilized by Beard was his emphasis on the physical nature of cooking. Accordingly, he stressed the importance of cooks learning to use their hands as tools. In *James Beard's Theory & Practice of Good Cooking* Beard refers to the hands as a cook's best tools. In an interview with Evan Jones (1978) Beard expressed his irritation with people who refuse to use their hands to touch food: "I can't stand prissy people who think there is something dirty about sticking fingers in food" (29). Moreover, he stressed the role of touch as a learning tool: "If you learn to fold egg whites into a mixture by using the side of your hand to cut down and the open palm to bring the mixture up, you quickly grasp the real technique of light, swift folding that doesn't deflate egg whites" (30).

The development of touch, according to Beard, can be applied to different cooking methods. For example, he insists that proper roasting is based, in part, on a cook's practiced eye and sensitive finger (Beard 1965). This narrative suggests that another element to learning cookery is kinesthetic. Good cooks learn through performance of tasks. It is likely that repetition also plays a role in this form of learning.

One goal Beard set for beginning cooks was to learn how to work "beyond" the use of recipes. In the same *People* magazine interview (Stewart 1981) Beard was asked if cooks should slavishly follow the directions of a recipe: "People ought to do something the way it's written once, and then branch out" (67). Thus, it seems that Beard wanted cooks to use recipes as guidelines or perhaps as starting points. In fact, in a later interview published in *U.S. News & World Report* (Stewart 1981), Beard insisted that recipes that are too specific have "killed" the adventure associated with cooking. By encouraging novice cooks to go beyond recipes, Beard also wanted them to develop a sense of trust in themselves. A consideration of the need to use the self—senses, imagination, information—in learning to cook may be the hallmark of Beard's teaching.

James Beard also stressed the potential for learning from mistakes in the kitchen. In an article written by food historian Betty Fussell (1983) Beard is quoted as emphasizing that mistakes are sources of learning and should not be regretted. Beard presented mistakes in such a way that students learned without feeling guilty. Evan Jones (1978) observed Beard providing student cooks with feedback. Here Beard comments on a hash that had been prepared by students: "[T]his corned beef hash is drier than it should be. Does anyone disagree?" Note that Beard focuses on the taste and attempts to provide a standard for this dish. He discusses various reasons for the dish's dryness and suggests additional cream as a possible remedy for the problem. It is thus important to create a social atmosphere that encourages experimentation and does not punish learners for committing mistakes.

In the sixties Beard became popular as a spokesperson for food and appliance manufacturers. The cooking school was named after him. The number of his publications increased considerably. It was also during this decade that Beard's health began to fail. Nevertheless, Beard continued to cook and teach throughout the seventies and also maintained a demanding writing schedule. Some of the books published under Beard's name during this decade include *James Beard's American Cookery* (1971), *Beard on Bread* (1973), and *James Beard's Theory & Practice of Good Cooking* (1977). By the end of the seventies Beard's failing health limited his travel and teaching. On January 23, 1984, he died at the age of eighty-one. It was only proper that Beard—who published over twenty books on food, wrote numerous articles, and taught countless aspiring cooks—earned the title "Dean of American Cuisine." Beard's biographer Robert Clark (1996) has summarized his lasting impact:

> Today it is clear that in a number of ways he moves among us, both in the works he left behind and as a presence not so very different from what he was in life. Of his twenty-two books, at least half remain in print, and many continue to enjoy significant sales. Restaurants and food purveyors still advertise endorsements or mentions he made of them a decade or more before. People frequently express surprise to hear he is dead; close friends and colleagues slip effortlessly and nearly without notice from past to present tense when they discuss him. (330)

Perhaps James Beard's legacy is that he discovered something in life that he truly loved. He affected the lives of his students, readers, and colleagues through his ability to both learn and teach and by sharing his devotion to the craft of cooking.

References

Beard, J. 1992. *Delights & Prejudices: A Memoir With Recipes.* 1964. New York: Manufacturers Hanover Trust Co.

———. 1977. *James Beard's Theory & Practice of Good Cooking.* Philadelphia, Pa.: Running Press.

———. 1965. "House & Garden's Roast Meat Cookbook." *House & Garden* 128: 229–31.

———. 1964. "Be Adventurous with Liqueurs." *House & Garden* 126: 218.

Bedford, C. 2004. "Healthy and Humane: The Floyd Boulevard Local Food Market." *Women, Food & Agriculture Network* 7 (2): 1, 4.

Clark, R. 1996. *The Solace of Food: A Life of James Beard.* South Royalton, Vt.: Steerforth Press.

David, E. 1980. *Elizabeth David Classics.* Newton, Mass.: Biscuit Books.

Erwitt, E. 1981. "What's to Come in American Cuisine: A Talk With Noted Food Authority James Beard." *House & Garden* 153: 151, 158.

Freiburger, A. 2004. "New Farmers' Market Is 'Values Added': Floyd Boulevard Local Foods Market in Sioux City, Iowa." *The Organic Broadcaster* 12, no. 5.

Fussell, B. 1983. "Great American Taste." *Redbook* 161: 78–80.

Halweil, B. 2003. "The Argument for Local Food." *World Watch* 16: 20–27.

Jones, E. 1990. *Epicurean Delight: The Life and Times of James Beard.* New York: Simon & Schuster.

———. 1978. "The Zest of James Beard." *New York Times*, December 24.

Kafka, B. 1992. Foreword to *Delights & Prejudices: A Memoir with Recipes.* New York: Manufacturers Hanover Trust Co.

Lefebvre, K. 2002. "Peace and Justice Advocate Concerned About Survival of Small Hog Farms." Accessed October 3, 2004, at http://www.catholicglobe.org/archive/2002/1002/03/stories/story7.htm.

McManus, R. 2004. "I Call It a Delicious Revolution." *Sierra* 89: 28–29.

Oregon Historical Society. Portland, Ore. 2005. http://www.ohs.org.

Rosman, J. 2005. "Humane Farmers' Market Seeks a Sustainable Future of Its Own. Humane Society of the United States." Accessed March 7, 2005, at http://www.hsus.org/farm _animals/farm_animals_news/humane_farmers_market_seeks_a_sustainable_future_of_its_own.html.

Skow, J. 1966. "Menus for Entertaining." *Saturday Evening Post* 239: 28–31.

Stewart, A. 1981. "James Beard, Emperor of Epicures, Cooks up a Whole New Culinary Regime." *People* 16: 65–67.

Wisdom, M. 2001. "Pressing the Fresh." *New Orleans Magazine* 35: 17.

M. F. K. Fisher

An Ongoing Conversation

It seems to me that our three basic needs, for food, security
and love, are so mixed and mingled and entwined that
we cannot straightly think of one without the others. So it
happens that when I write about hunger, I am really writing
about love and hunger for it, and warmth and the hunger
for it, and warmth and the love of it and the hunger for it . . .
and then the warmth and richness and fine reality of hunger
satisfied . . . and it is all one.
—M. F. K. Fisher, *The Gastronomical Me*

MARY FRANCES KENNEDY FISHER lived a life that defied cat-
egorization. She certainly wrote about food and eating. However,
when she wrote about food, she invariably touched on many different subjects: the pleasures of appetite, of love, and how to feel
at home anywhere. In the words of David Lazar (1992), while food
was invariably the central theme of her writing, Mary Frances always
managed to "transcend the subject" (xi). It seems that the more I
read Fisher, the more I learn about myself and my relationship with
food—my wants, desires, needs, memories and fantasies.

I had hoped to learn more about this person, who has been referred to as the "Grand [*sic*] Dame of Gastronomy" (Scott 1977),
the "Philosopher-Poet of the Stove" (Fussell 1983b), and whom W.
H. Auden called "America's greatest writer" (O'Neill 1992). It was

Ruth Reichl's words about Fisher, however, that helped me to begin to understand her achievement. In an article published in *Gourmet* magazine Reichl (1999) recalled several interviews she had conducted with her for *Ms.* magazine in the seventies. In her article Reichl described the work of individuals such as Julia Child and James Beard, who dedicated themselves to teaching people about food, and Craig Claiborne, who told us where and what to eat. However, it was Fisher who emphasized the need to learn how to talk about and experience food. She showed us that there is always much more occurring when we break bread and drink wine together. For me this conversation remains an ongoing process. In order to understand my relationship with food, I must also engage in a process of self-observation, understanding, and (hopefully) change.

M. F. K. Fisher (née Mary Frances Kennedy) was born in Albion, Michigan, on July 3, 1908 (Reardon 1994), the oldest child of Edith and Rex Kennedy. Rex insisted that had Mary Frances waited another day to arrive, she would have been named Independencia. While the family still resided in Albion, Mary Frances was followed by a sister, Anne.

Rex and his brother, Walter, had moved to Albion in 1904 to purchase and manage the *Albion Recorder,* which had just become a daily publication. They were the fourth generation of newspapermen in the Kennedy family (Eames 1981).

When Mary Frances was three years old, Rex sold his share of the newspaper to Walter and the family moved to the West Coast. This decision was, in part, a form of rebellion against his family's insistence on traditional career paths in journalism for its children (Reardon 1994). After failed attempts at beachcombing on Puget Sound and managing an orange grove, Rex returned to the publishing business and purchased the *Whittier Daily News,* based in Whittier, California (Storace 1989), where he served as its editor for forty-two years (Passic 1993). At the time Whittier was an insular community of Quakers, far removed from the rich cultural life of Portland experienced by James Beard or the fascinating social gumbo of Mobile observed by Eugene Walter. The Episcopal Kennedy family was therefore an oddity (Storace 1989). (Coincidentally, the Nixon family made Whittier its home a few years later, where Richard Milhous Nixon, the thirty-seventh president of the United States, would attend college.)

The Kennedy family lived on a sprawling parcel of land complete with an orchard (Acocella 1998). The family increased in size when a sister, Nora, was born in 1917, and a brother, David, followed in 1919. Mary Frances and her siblings were surrounded by orange groves and vineyards. The family grew most of its produce and raised pigeons, turkeys, a pig, and a cow (Fussell 1983b). Their fresh produce and other foods were typically served with homemade bread and locally produced butter (Villas 1978). This lifestyle was reminiscent of James Beard's boyhood in Oregon, where his parents sought out locally produced foods, such as dairy products from the Tillamook Valley. Similarly, many of Fisher's early recollections centered around food and tastes, such as the hot fuzz her grandmother skimmed off a steaming pot of strawberry jam (Eames 1981).

It is not surprising, therefore, that at a very early age Fisher learned to cook. She recalled feeling at home in the kitchen, constantly stirring one thing or another. In fact, Fisher later wrote that she learned quickly that cooking was an excellent way for her to get attention from her family (1990). Naturally falling into the role of cook's helper, at an early age she produced meals for the family on the cook's night off. Later in life she remarked that her work in the kitchen provided her with a sense of power, a feeling she loved (Fussell 1983b). Arlene Voski Avakian (1997) would later write passionately about cooking and food as ways for women both to communicate with each other and to experience a sense of independence.

These early experiences with food and cooking had a substantial impact on Fisher. Like James Beard, her early memories are frequently revealed in her later writing. Examples of this include her recollection of eating fresh peach pie with her father and sister in their Model T enroute to Whittier (Davidhoff 1982), as well as sleeping out after barbecues with lariats coiled around them to ward off snakes (Fussell 1983b). Her lifestyle during this period was reminiscent of the young James Beard (born only a few years earlier), whose fondest memories included hunting for and cooking razor clams on the beach and helping his mother grill whole salmon over an open fire.

Like Beard, Julia Child, Elizabeth David, and many other creative individuals, Fisher grew up in a family of strong-willed, articulate individuals who held deep-seated and often conflicting opinions about many topics, including food. Moreover, Fisher was also strongly influenced by a powerful matriarchal family system (Fussell 1983b). These women included her mother and her maternal grandmother, who had moved in with the family after her husband died (Gioia 1998). Mrs. Holbrook was a Campbellite, a religious sect whose members also called themselves Disciples of Christ. The church promoted strict dietary guidelines that were partially influenced by W. K. Kellogg of Battle Creek, Michigan.

Grandmother Holbrook, in particular, dominated the kitchen—with her boiled dressings poured over wet, shredded lettuce, and custards (Angelou 1983)—as well as the dinner table. Yet she also preached about the importance of simple foods. Later remarks by Fisher reflected this same understanding. For example, she felt that meat hashed with a knife is far more flavorful than when it is "mauled in a food processor" (Villas 1978). Fisher would probably have agreed with Father Dominic Garramone that the bread accompanying the hash tasted better when made with one's hands than with a bread machine.

As the editor of the local paper, Rex was a prolific writer and a dedicated journalist. It is not surprising, therefore, that like other members of her family Fisher seems to have had a natural talent for writing. It was through her work with her father at the newspaper that she began to develop her writing skills. At an early age she was substituting for different writers, such as the editor of the society column. This early apprenticeship helped her develop the ability to meet deadlines, since her copy was always due at 1:00 P.M. (Storace 1989).

Fisher was also a voracious reader and compared her habit with that of an addict, reading from morning to night (Reardon 1994). In her biographical study of Fisher, Joan Reardon would later remark that it was no accident that Mary Frances was "literate, opinionated and dedicated to her craft" (27).

In Whittier a relatively rigid social system favored Quakers and relegated the Episcopalians to second-class social status. Catholics and Jews were placed even lower on the social scale (Fisher 1970). The Episcopalian Fishers consequently did not fit in well with the local culture. In order to develop a sense of place in the community, Fisher's mother worked for a women's club and a small mission that "would later become the Episcopalian church" (121), while Rex reluctantly joined the Masons. Unfortunately, although Whittier did not offer the same level of social life available in the larger cities, the family had enough resources to dine out at excellent restaurants, which helped develop an appreciation for good food in the young Mary Frances.

Fisher enrolled in several public schools in Whittier and later attended a college preparatory boarding school. She yearned to escape small-town California and spent a single semester at Illinois College in Jacksonville finding it equally stifling (Angelou 1983). A small, conservative community located in rural Illinois just outside Springfield, Jacksonville was probably not substantially different from Whittier. Fisher subsequently spent a semester at Whittier College. Back in California, she made the acquaintance of Alfred Young Fisher. They had met at UCLA and, according to Fisher, both wanted to escape their shared small-town heritage (Eames 1981). For Mary Fisher in particular, the move away with Al represented both a break from Grandmother Holbrook's cooking and the Quakers of Whittier.

Dennis Getto

Celebrating Local Foods and Traditions

Growing up in Wisconsin, and in a household that subscribed to the daily Milwaukee *Journal* (and later the Milwaukee *Journal-Sentinel*), Milwaukee was always the exemplar of big-city sophistication for us. The best restaurants and most exotic foods were in Milwaukee. But there were also great restaurants across Wisconsin: Door County, West Bend, the Fox Valley and the Kettle Moraine region. And it was Dennis Getto who brought these feasts to our family room.
—Mark Schaub (e-mail message to author, March 7, 2005)

Intensely conservative and WASP, Elmhurst, Illinois, in the fifties and sixties was a place where ethnic foods did not extend far beyond several pizzerias and a chop suey house. It was also a place where the condiment shelf of the typical family's refrigerator sported little more than ketchup, yellow mustard, and Worcestershire sauce, prompting the joke that a marriage had been longstanding if the couple were "into their second bottle of Tabasco sauce." Submerged in uniform gastronomic blandness, this was hardly a region similar to that of James Beard's childhood. Yet it was where an interesting and imaginative food writer named Dennis Getto grew up. Like M. F. K. Fisher, Getto developed an appreciation for, as well as a talent to write about, ordinary foods offered up by numerous restaurants and cafés, and not just those that serve their fare on white linen tablecloths.

There are numerous restaurant critics affiliated with newspapers and other publications across the United States. For readers like Mark Schaub, however, Dennis Getto provides more than just information on restaurants in his region. He also reflects the interesting food traditions that can be discovered in countless places throughout Wisconsin. Whether it involves where to find a great bowl of chili after a Packers game (Getto 1997) or Wisconsin-style barbecue on the banks of the Mississippi River, Getto is always ready to present his readers with interesting recommendations as a way for people to expand their horizons and "experience the world in a pleasant way."

Dennis Getto grew up in a small Italian American family in the western suburbs of Chicago. As with Father Dom, Getto was strongly influenced by his mother's cooking, which combined family traditions from Calabria with what she learned from watching a Chicago television series called *Creative Cookery* that featured Francois Pope. He watched her make pastries and "work the pans." Thus, at an early age Getto was helping to make stocks and sauces. By age ten he was already preparing meals for the family.

As he matured, Getto continued to cook. He was influenced by a French instructor in college who would invite students to visit an authentic French restaurant in downtown Chicago once a semester. Participants had to abide by two basic rules: they were expected to pay for their own meals, and they were only permitted to speak French.

Inspired, in part, by his trips to French restaurants in Chicago, Getto continued to develop his cooking skills. He visited French-speaking Canada and aspired to make his own croissants, as well as other French foods. He then picked up Curnonsky's *Larousse Gastronomique,* a complicated culinary reference book by an author whose nom de plume was based on the Latin for "Why not?" When the culinary encyclopedia became too complex, Getto resorted to the process of trial and error. After all, there were no fishermen in Elmhurst to provide fish carcasses for making court bouillon!

Getto continued to cook throughout his undergraduate years. He attended graduate school at Marquette University, where he studied journalism. During this period Getto continued to learn about cooking. He enrolled in classes with Myra Dorros, a student of Madeline Kamman. Like many others before him, he traveled to France, where he attended classes taught by Simone Beck, Julia Child's colleague and coauthor. He later studied with Giuliano Bugialli, Julia Child, and Jacques Pepin. More recently, Getto accompanied Rick Bayless and company to visit Vera Cruz and Oaxaca in Mexico.

Getto graduated from Marquette University with a master's degree in journalism, and in 1982 he began work at the Milwaukee *Journal* as the restaurant critic. His column at the *Journal* (and later at the combined *Journal Sentinel*) has rapidly expanded beyond the realm of restaurant reviews. For example, in 2000 Getto reviewed *The Farmer's Market Cookbook* (Ruben 2000). In his review he emphasized the importance of farmers' markets and the value of cooking according to the seasons (Getto 2003). In yet another article he wrote a eulogy for a local restaurateur who had popularized Cajun food in the Milwaukee area (Getto 2001b). In another piece he took the time to describe a way to cook chicken with a can of beer in its cavity (Getto 2001a).

Whether visiting great tents at summer festivals in Milwaukee, tasting charcoal roasted chicken on the shores of Lake Geneva (Getto 2000), or enjoying a good hot dog in Madison, Getto consistently celebrates local specialties, such as bratwurst or fried perch caught the same day and sautéed in butter. He strives to discover eateries where local cooks prepare good food using fresh, regional ingredients, irrespective of whether they are served on fine china or wrapped in newspaper. It is not just haute cuisine that attracts the attention of Dennis Getto.

For readers such as Mark Schaub, Dennis Getto keeps a firm grip on both palate and wallet. He is not so much interested in telling people where to eat but where they can celebrate good food, tradition, and camaraderie. Forget the chain restaurants. You'll be much happier dining in a locally owned supper club recommended by this maverick food critic.

Al and Mary Frances Kennedy Fisher were married in 1929. After less than two weeks of marriage, they (like Julia Child and her husband Paul) set sail for France, traveling third class. Al had been awarded a fellowship, and the couple moved to Dijon, France, where he completed his doctorate in English literature (Angelou 1983; Reardon 1994). Mary also pursued her studies, including drawing and sculpture (Reardon 1994).

Like Julia Child and Elizabeth David, Fisher's experiences in France constituted an epiphany. French became her second language (Angelou 1983). She discovered French culture and writers such as Colette (Reardon 1994). This was, in a sense, a form of cultural and intellectual immersion. She threw herself into this process. Writing to her sister Anne at one point during her stay in France, she remarked: "It's thrilling, fascinating, marvelous—and it gets better and better" (11). She spoke of lamplighters and hot chestnuts sold on street corners, as well as wines, restaurants, and small, intimate cafés. This immersion process has also been described as a form of culinary seduction that also shaped the lives of such cooks as Julia Child and Alice Waters (Reardon 1994). For these and many others, France became a place "where the abiding pleasures of food and wine, gastronomy, and a well-documented history of cuisine are fatal attractions" (3). It is important to stress that this exposure was not limited solely to cooking and dining but included the essential components of a truly grand cuisine, namely, ingredients, procedures, history, and traditions.

In addition to helping her husband complete his doctoral studies, Fisher shopped at the markets, cooked, sketched, and wrote. Eventually she earned a bachelor's degree from the University of Dijon. For a young woman—even from California, with its bountiful food choices—France must have been an eye-opening experience. The wide assortment of foods found at markets in Europe is hardly replicated in the United States. The French, for example, claim that they produce so many types of cheeses that one can eat a different one every day of the year without repeating. Moreover, the French and other Europeans are hardly modest about proclaiming the joys of the table—something that would never have been broadcast through the social circles of Whittier. The preparation of meals by Fisher for Alfred and their guests was regarded as a highly creative process. Her overarching goal was to enable her guests to "forget their homes" while dining with her and Alfred (Reardon 1994).

Although cooking in the limited facilities offered by a boarding house was challenging. Fisher was up to the task. To a degree she faced the same challenges as Julia Child, who, while living with Paul in Paris, prepared meals on a small stove for their guests. We can see evidence of Julia Child's kitchen in France in the photograph on the cover of Noel Riley Fitch's biography, *Appetite for Life*, which shows a lanky Child stooping over a small gas stove slightly larger than one we might find in a camping trailer. Not only did she use it to produce food for Paul and their guests but she eventually conducted cooking classes with the same equipment.

One distinct advantage of entertaining guests with good food was that Fisher helped create a social group of intellectuals, many of whom were writers. By interacting within this group, she continued to develop her own writing skills. She kept a diary and corresponded with a number of friends and family members back in the United States.

In 1932 the Fishers moved back to California, where they returned to a country in the grip of the Great Depression. The Kennedys provided the couple with a place to stay. Employment was scarce, so they accepted part-time jobs until Al finally landed a teaching position at Occidental College located in Eagle Rock, a suburb of Los Angeles. It was during this period that she published her first article, for which she received thirty-five dollars for the illustrations plus text (Reardon 1994).

While Al taught at the college, Fisher worked part-time in an art shop and spent her time off in the local public library. One day she impulsively picked up a book of Elizabethan recipes that had been left on a table by another patron (Villas 1978). She found the recipes and stories about food fascinating and soon was spending more and more time in the library, where she read a wide range of books on food and cookery. It was at this time that she met George Dillwyn Parrish. The latter was a creative type, the son of parents who were both painters. He was also a cousin of Maxwell Parrish, the celebrated illustrator who had already created a highly successful career for himself (Reardon 1994). This meeting would, in due course, shape the rest of her life.

Fisher soon began to write essays about food based on her readings as well as her experiences. At first her writing simply provided a source of amusement for herself, her husband, and a few friends (Villas 1978). Eventually she would sign her work "M.F.K. Fisher," following the style of her mother, who signed her checks E.O.H. Kennedy (Reardon, 1994).

When Fisher subsequently showed her writings to her husband, she also included their friends Gigi and Dillwyn Parrish. In addition to being an accomplished writer, Parrish, like Paul Child, was adept at sketching. In fact, he had already collaborated with his sister, Anne, on two children's books, with each supplying both the written text and the illustrations. They also worked together to create a book of sketches, *Lustres*, which was published in 1924.

Gigi and Dillwyn Parrish passed Fisher's essays on to Anne Parrish, who showed them to her editor at Harper's. Anne was a successful writer who, at the time of her death in 1957, had published nineteen works and had garnered a Harper Prize in 1925. Her support of Fisher's work was therefore quite helpful. These essays eventually coalesced into Fisher's first book, *Serve It Forth* (1937b).

After Gigi and Dillwyn Parrish separated, he moved back to his family's home on the East Coast. Fisher continued to send him her work and corresponded with him on a regular basis. He provided her with both feedback and encouragement. In a manner reminiscent of Paul and Julia Child's relationship as well as the liaison between Elizabeth David and Norman Douglas, Dillwyn Parrish served Fisher as mentor, confidant, and friend.

In 1936 Parrish and his mother invited Fisher to join them on an extended trip to Europe. With her husband's agreement, Fisher journeyed to England to meet with the publishers of *Serve It Forth*. The editors at Harper and Brothers certainly must have been shocked when they discovered that "M. F. K. Fisher" was not a man but an attractive, fashionably dressed woman. Later, in the United States, Lucius Beebe, the columnist who helped James Beard's catering company achieve success, complained that M.F.K. was a woman (Lazar 1992).

From England they traveled on to France and then to Switzerland. It was in Switzerland that Fisher first visited a small stone cottage and vineyard overlooking Geneva that had been purchased by Parrish and his sister. Located near Le Paquis, it was to become a literary and artistic community for the Parrishes and their group of friends, which included the Fishers.

When *Serve It Forth* was published in 1937, it received positive reviews, including one from S. I. Hayakawa (Reardon 1994). Here Fisher introduces the reader to a variety of approaches to food and eating that have been adopted by different writers. However, as she later stated in *The Art of Eating*, she intends to write about eating, what to eat, and people who eat (1990). What ensues—or is served forth—is a collection of interesting essays that draws the reader into a consideration of her relationship with food and that covers a broad spectrum of topics, both historical and anecdotal.

For example, in one essay amounting to slightly less than three pages, Fisher takes the reader into a borderland filled with secret things people like to eat. She draws them into her hotel room—which they had visited in order to escape the bitter cold of their cramped, dirty apartment that February in Strasbourg. The room is seductive—spacious and well lit, with windows covered by billowy curtains (1990). And after her husband returns to work, they remain alone with Fisher.

She sets the stage by describing a bone-chilling wind outside the window. The maid has long since gone, papers have been delivered, and tangerine sections have grown plump on pieces of newspaper draped over the radiator. Soon the sections of tangerine are gone, with Fisher wondering what makes them "so magical": How can such a simple food be so special? Is it the crackle of the crisp surrounding membrane, the rush of cool pulp, or the perfume? Fisher admits she really cannot tell. The reader, however, can faintly sense the magic of the experience after spending this time with Fisher.

Nearly forty years later, Nancy Scott (1977) wrote about a similar experience with Fisher. In her article Scott proclaimed that no other cook could turn an innocent melon into "a gothic anecdote." Betty Fussell's (1983b) words echoed this sentiment when she claimed that no one else could evoke such complex and rich images of something as simple as mashed potatoes and ketchup. It is hardly surprising that this slim book, reprinted a number of times, has been described by writers such as David Eames (1981) as "fat with scholarship, opinion, anecdote, humor" (38).

It was during this period that Fisher asked her husband to leave her. She had fallen deeply in love with Parrish, and her relationship with Al had become strained. He returned to the United States and accepted a teaching position at Smith College, where he later became dean of the English department there (Reichl 1981).

It was summer in Switzerland, and Fisher and Parrish, who she fondly called Timmy, moved into the small stone cottage near Le Paquis. They gardened and tended to the grapevines, ate fried tomatoes, and drank beer chilled in their fountain (Reardon 1994). This place was, according to Betty Fussell (1983b), where Fisher learned about "the power of food to evoke our senses" (26).

While continuing to write in Switzerland, Fisher returned to the United States to inform her parents that she planned to divorce Al Fisher. Her parents supported her decision and Fisher filed the necessary papers before returning to Parrish in Switzerland (Reardon 1994). Her return was heralded by blossoming violets and wildflowers as well as the growth of new grapevines. Their life together became one subject of her writing as she described eating what they had grown or preserved (Greene 1986). Amid the growth and promise of spring, Fisher's sister Nora and brother David had planned to spend the summer with her and Parrish, but Parrish developed a sudden embolism in his leg that necessitated several surgeries and eventual amputation (Reardon 1994). As his health deteriorated, Parrish and Fisher spent more and more time in hospitals and clinics. As Elizabeth David and her lover were setting sail for the Mediterranean on the *Evelyn Hope*, optimism was fading for Fisher and Parrish. They returned to California by sea and were married in a civil ceremony. The couple subsequently purchased ninety acres of land near Helmet, California, with the intention of rebuilding a small home on the property (Reardon 1994). The next two years were punctuated by trips to various clinics, where Parrish was finally diagnosed as having a progressive, incurable illness called Buerger's disease, an acute inflammation and clotting of arteries and veins (Center 1998–2004).

During this period Fisher began to write essays on the oyster, an unassuming mollusk. These essays served as the basis for her slender book *Consider the Oyster* (1941), which was published shortly after Parrish committed suicide and which she dedicated to him. Beginning with the sexual ambiguity of the mollusk, Fisher writes: "Almost any normal oyster never knows from one year to the next whether he is he or she" (1990 125). She then guides the reader through a series of seductive essays. She discusses eating oysters, as well as the aphrodisiac qualities of the mollusk. She dispenses recipes throughout the book on topics like how to roast oysters or create an oyster stew. The book concludes with an essay that recommends beverages to be served with oysters.

Following Parrish's death, Fisher returned to her family in Whittier. At her mother's recommendation, she joined Nora, David, and his pregnant wife, Sarah, in Guadalajara, Mexico (Reardon 1994). Later that year her brother also committed suicide (Angelou 1983), the day before he was to be inducted into the army (Lazar 1992).

Despite such personal tragedies, Fisher continued to write. She completed *How to Cook a Wolf* in 1942 and *The Gastronomical Me* the following year. *How to Cook a Wolf*, which was dictated to her sister Nora (Reardon 1994), was published at a time when housewives were saving items such as tinfoil and newspaper for the war effort (Taylor 1948). In a style similar to that of Elizabeth David, who wrote in postwar England, Fisher offered ways in which American cooks could deal with the austerities of rationing—how to keep the wolf at the door at bay. For example, she elevated such dishes as scrambled eggs to the level of satisfying and comforting foods.

There is also a sense of humor present in this book. Fisher's tongue-in-cheek set of guidelines includes how to not boil an egg, in which she provides the reader with a few recipes for different egg dishes, as well as an abbreviated discourse on different styles of omelets, including French, soufflé, Italian frittata, and Asian foo yeung. Underlying her essays was the premise that thinking about, remembering, and writing about food during times of trouble constituted a form of spiritual nourishment (Rosofsky 2004). Fisher's advice, moreover, also reflects a basic tenet in her writing, namely, the importance of maintaining a thoughtful and sensitive relationship with food. The degree of sensitivity increases during shortages, and Fisher chides those people who are shamefully careless with the food they eat: "When we exist without thought or thanksgiving we are not men, but beasts" (1990). Her writing promotes a sense of "stalwart resistance" to the vagaries resulting from wartime rationing (Rosofsky 2004).

In 1943 Fisher discovered she was pregnant with daughter Anne Kennedy Parrish (Reardon 2004). Several years later she met and later married producer Donald Fried, with whom she had a second daughter, Kennedy Fried, in 1946 (Angelou 1983). She continued to write articles for a variety of magazines such as *The New Yorker*, and wrote screenplays for Paramount in Hollywood. In 1947 she began to work on a translation of (Jean) Anselme Brillat-Savarin's *Physiology of Taste*, which was published in 1949. Although the book, originally written in 1825, had already been translated into English by several writers, Fisher's edition received a very favorable review in the *New York Times* (Fisher 1949). Early in the book we come across an interesting aphorism that resonates strongly with Fisher's own writing: "Animals feed themselves; men eat; but only wise men know the art of eating" (1949, 3). During this period Fisher also published *Here Let Us Feast: A Book of Banquets* (1946), *Not Now, But Now* (1947), and *An Alphabet for Gourmets* (1949).

In 1951 Rex Kennedy died. When he and his family had moved to Whittier, the locals gave them a single year to make it or depart. It was to be over forty years later that Rex died within a few blocks of the newspaper he had edited all those years. Several years later Fisher divorced Fried, stating that he had been more trouble than the children. In 1953 Fisher took her two daughters, Anne and Kennedy, to France, where she developed material to write a book about this experience, *Map of Another Town: A Memoir* (Fussell 1983). They spent nearly a year together in France.

In 1961 she again returned to France for an extended stay, during which she collaborated with the then recently published cookery writer Julia Child and Michael Field in editing Time-Life's *Cooking of Provencial France* (Hawes 1983). The book was published in 1968.

In the early seventies Fisher moved into a home she had designed in Glen Ellen, California, situated on the land of a friend (Lazar 1992). In Fisher's later years her house reflected a rich and inviting lifestyle. The simple structure was set on a ranch in Sonoma country, California, in the heart of a great wine-producing region. Numerous writers felt compelled to describe the three-room home as though nobody else has done it justice. However, the central themes of Fisher's lifestyle in that home revolved around a simple approach to life, not just cooking. The great room where she cooked and conducted numerous interviews with journalists and friends was devoid of gadgets and convenience foods. She embodied Father Dom's belief in close physical contact with food by utilizing tools such as bowls and knives in lieu of food processors and blenders. Moreover, when Fisher entertained in this room, she also prepared simple meals. Despite this, many of her guests proclaimed it was the best food they had ever eaten.

The welcoming sense of Fisher's lifestyle permeates her writing. She possesses a knack for engaging the reader in an intimate conversation about something as simple as a meal enjoyed in a restaurant. In an early essay (Fisher 1937a) she describes a restaurant she visited while alone on a long hike. She enters and discovers that she is the only patron. It was an "old mill which a Parisian chef had bought and turned into one of France's most famous restaurants, and my mad waitress was the only servant" (737).

The meal she enjoys becomes an intimate experience between

her and the reader/confidant. Early during the meal, Fisher orders a bottle of wine, sharing her chagrin over that indiscretion with the reader: "What a fool, I thought, to order a whole bottle. I'm a fool here all alone and with more miles to walk before I reach Avallon and my fresh clothes and a bed" (738). Nevertheless, she settles back into her chair and savors the moment, which includes a cat purring under the ferns.

As one course is succeeded by another, we enjoy not only her description of the food but also her relationship with the "mad waitress." The latter delivers the hors d'oeuvres on eight different plates and watches as Fisher eats, suggesting: "Perhaps Madame would care to start with the pickled herring? It is not like any other" (739). While Fisher dug into several of the small fillets, she looked up and saw that the waitress had stopped breathing. The latter asked her is she was pleased, and Fisher said yes, upon which the waitress quietly pushed a plate of sizzling endive toward her and disappeared.

The impact of this essay does not result from the fact that Fisher was dining in a famous restaurant. Rather, she is able to direct our attention to details that might otherwise go unnoticed. For example, she talks about her fascination with the way the waitress uncorks a vintage wine. She does not follow the prescribed tradition involving "exaggerated precautions against touching, tipping, or jarring the bottle" (739) but instead handles the bottle nonchalantly. Fisher quietly describes how the waitress struggles with a stubborn cork: "The cork was very tight, and I thought for a minute she would break it" (739). The reader's stomach tenses as the waitress slowly works out the cork and wipes the lip of the bottle. We breathe a sigh of relief as the waitress pours an inch of wine into a glass, turns her back to Fisher and, like a priest taking communion, gulps it down.

In the course of just a few minutes Fisher has slowed time to illustrate something we might normally take for granted: a waitress opening a bottle of wine. Just as Dennis Getto shares his delight in finding a great fish fry during the Lenten season and Father Dom proclaims the inherent delight in kneading dough, Fisher demonstrates how the simplest aspects of life can become engaging.

Perhaps Fisher's greatest gift is her ability to reflect a fully engaged and vibrant lifestyle. She shared this lifestyle with her readers over the course of decades. She survived many personal tragedies, including the deaths of loved ones and several divorces. For example, in her "Swiss Journal"(1988) she describes her painful coexistence with Parrish's debilitating illness: "I look up to see in the mirror above my washstand if there is a light reflected from Dillwyn's room. We tried two pills tonight, and that did no good, and then gave the old faithful shot of Analgeticum at 8:00. He is asleep, heavily, with his mouth dropped askew. I am fairly sure that by 12:00 he will call me. Then it will be Pantopon" (129).

Finances were always a challenge for Fisher as she single-handedly raised two daughters. Her royalties for publications rarely rose above five hundred dollars (Reed 1986), and her books never sold well (Lazar 1992). Nevertheless, she claims that she was always able to keep the wolf from the door.

As she aged, Fisher also taught us how to remain alive and energetic throughout our lives. Her written output continued until she was unable to write or type up her own work. At that point she hired someone to type as she dictated.

Part of the full life Fisher espoused included her thoughtful relationship with food. The latter quality has, at times, been identified as an important facet of contemporary American life. "People," we are told, "are more conscious of their nutrition." Were she alive today, Fisher might point to the problem that much of our dietary information is provided in advertising, which sends mixed messages to consumers: Expunge carbs. Eliminate fat. Be thin. Eat what you want. Shun eggs. The super size costs only an additional thirty-nine cents. Avoid beef. Eat hearty when you are celebrating. And don't feel guilty about eating too much as long as the food is fat-free.

The aging Fisher was beautifully captured by numerous writers: a "physical knockout at 60" (Reed 1986); "as sensual as mocha cheesecake at 74" (Angelou 1983); and "remarkably beautiful, if somewhat fragile, in her eighth decade" (Greene 1986). However, her greatest gift to us during that period of her life was to describe the aging process from the standpoint of an active and engaged person (Fisher 1964). This is a challenge we all must face as we follow Fisher into eternity.

References

Acocella, J. 1998. "Feasting on Life." *The New Yorker* 74: 172–77.

Angelou, M. 1983. "M. F. K. Fisher." *People* 19: 63.

Center, J. H. V. 1998–2004. "Types of Vasculitis, The Johns Hopkins Vasculitis Center." Accessed August 10, 2004, at http://www.vasculitis.ned.jhu.edu/typesof/Buergers.html.

Davidhoff, R. 1982. "Fisher: Past, Present and Future Together." *Los Angeles Times* September: 8: 10–11.

Eames, D. 1981. "How to Cook a Life." *Quest* 5: 38–42.

Fisher, M. F. K. 1937a. "I Was Really Hungry." *The Atlantic Monthly* 159: 737–42.

———. 1937b. *Serve It Forth.* London: Harper and Brothers.

———.1941. *Consider the Oyster.* New York: Duell, Sloan & Pearce.

———.1942. *How to Cook a Wolf.* New York: Duell, Sloan & Pearce.

———. 1946. *Let Us Feast: A Book of Banquets.* New York: Viking.

———. 1947. *Not Now, But Now.* New York: Viking.

———. 1949. *An Alphabet for Gourmets.* New York: Viking.

———. 1949. *M. F. K. Fisher's Translation of the "Physiology of Taste."* New York: Alfred A. Knopf.

———. 1954. *The Gastronomical Me.* New York: Duell, Sloan & Pearce.

———. 1964. *Map of Another Town: A Memoir of Province.* Boston, Mass.: Little Brown.

———. 1964. *Sister Age.* New York: Alfred A. Knopf.

———. 1970. *Among Friends.* New York: Alfred A. Knopf.

———. 1988. "Swiss Journal." *Antaeus* 61: 129–46.

———. 1990. *The Art of Eating.* New York: John Wiley.

Fussell, B. 1983a. "Great American Taste." *Redbook* 161: 78–80.

———. 1983b. "M. F. K. Fisher: Philosopher-Poet of the Stove." In *Masters of American Cookery.* New York: Times Books.

Getto, D. 1997. *Great Wisconsin Restaurants: 101 Fabulous Choices by the*

Milwaukee Journal Sentinel's Restaurant Critic. Madison, Wis.: Trails
Media Group.

———. 2000. "Popeye's Knows How to Char-Roast Meats." *Journal Sentinel* June 15. Accessed October 2, 2004, at http://www.jsonline.com/dd/dining/junoo/gettco/18061500.asp.

———. 2001a. "Beer Can Chicken? This Is No Joke." *Journal Sentinel* September 5. Accessed October 4, 2004, at http://www.findarticles.com/p/articles/mi_gn4196/is_20010905/ai_n10719098.

———. 2001b. "Jolly Was Dedicated to Food, Fun and Charity." *Journal Sentinel* August 15. Accessed October 2, 2004, at http://www.jsonline.com/onwisconsin/dining/aug01/jolly15081401.asp.

———. 2003. "Markets Near and Far Offer Fresh Ideas." *Journal Sentinel* July 15. Accessed October 6, 2004, at http://wwwljsonline.com/entree/cooking/july03/155166.asp.

Gioia, D. 1998. *A Welcoming Life: The M. F. K. Fisher Scrapbook.* Washington, D.C., Counterpoint.

Greene, B. 1986. "America's Finest Food Writer—M. F. K. Fisher: An Intimate Portrait." *Food & Wine* 9: 28, 32.

Hawes, E. 1983. "M. F. K. Fisher: A Profile." *Gourmet* 43: 50, 53.

Lazar, D., ed. 1992. *Conversations with M. F. K. Fisher.* Jackson: University Press of Mississippi.

O'Neill, M. 1992. "M.F.K. Fisher, Writer on the Art of Food and the Taste of Living Is Dead at 83." *New York Times* June 24, late ed.

Passic, F. 1993. "M. F. K. Fisher." *Morning Star.* 2004. Accessed August 13, 2004, at http://www.albionmich.com/history/histor_notebook/930329.shtml.

Reardon, J. 1994. *M. F. K. Fisher, Julia Child and Alice Waters: Celebrating Pleasures of the Table.* New York: Random House.

———. 2004. *Poet of the Appetites: The Lives and Loves of M. F. K. Fisher.* New York: North Point Press.

Reed, J. 1986. "Eating Well Is the Best Revenge: A Conversation with M. F. K. Fisher." *U.S. News and World Report* 101: 62.

Reichl, R. 1981. "M. F. K. Fisher: How to Cook a Wolf and Other Gastronomic Feats." *Ms* 9: 90–91.

———. 1999. "A Sensual Hunger." *Gourmet* 59: 112.

Rosofsky, M. 2004. "Writing the Wolf Away: Food Meaning & Memories from World War II." *Food, Culture & Society* 7 (1): 47–58.

Ruben, R. 2000. *The Farmer's Market Cookbook.* New York: Lyons Press.

Scott, N. 1977. "The Grand Dame of Gastronomy." *San Francisco Sunday Chronicle-Examiner*, 22.

Storace, P. 1989. "The Art of M. F. K. Fisher." *New York Review of Books* 36: 42–45.

Taylor, H. 1948. "M. F. K. Fisher." *Wilson Library Bulletin* 23: 284.

Villas, J. 1978. "A Country Lunch with M. F. K. Fisher." *Bon Appetit* 23: 127–28.

Voski Avakian, A., ed. 1997. *Through the Kitchen Window: Women Explore the Intimate Meaning of Food and Cooking.* Boston:, Beacon Press.

Paul and Julia Child

Mastering More Than the Art of French Cooking

> No one thinks it's silly to invest two hours' work
> in two minutes' enjoyment; but if cooking is
> evanescent, well, so is the ballet.
> —Julia Child, as quoted in James Simpson,
> *Simpson's Contemporary Quotations*

FOR MANY PEOPLE in the United States, Julia Child was the embodiment of good cooking, eating, and conviviality. Over a period of years, armies of her fans and devotees—dubbed JWs (Julie Watchers) by her late husband, Paul (Riley Fitch 1997)—watched her on television, listened to her on the radio, and purchased her books, audiotapes, and videos. They traded stories of their favorite programs on *The French Chef,* imitated her falsetto voice, and waited in long lines—clutching gravy-stained copies of *Mastering the Art of French Cooking*—for her autograph.

The evolution of Julia Carolyn McWilliams into a cultural icon has spanned decades and crossed several continents. However, few people realize that as a young woman Julia McWilliams had little interest in what happened in the kitchen. Even fewer people recognize how the intertwined lives of Julia and Paul Child helped create the public persona we know today.

Julia Child was born on August 15, 1912, in Pasadena, California (Riley Fitch 1997). She was the firstborn child of John and Caro

McWilliams. Child's parents, like James Beard's, were socially active (Riley Fitch 1997). Their lifestyle included membership in a variety of private clubs. The family dined out frequently, and Child could even remember a dinner they had in Tijuana, Mexico, in which she watched Caesar Cardini, the inventor of the Caesar salad, prepare his creation at their table.

Even though the family ate well, Child's mother did not cook often. Usually Caro limited her cooking to the maid's days off (Child 1999). Child described the food her family consumed as being good, plain New England food. She also described her mother's cooking as being limited to Welsh rarebit and baking-powder biscuits (Coffey 1988).

Child's formal education began when she was enrolled in a Montessori school. She then attended Polytechnic school through grade nine. In high school Child was sent to the Katherine Branson School, a boarding school, where she completed a college prep education course of study. While at Branson, Child exhibited an interest in the theater and writing. After completing high school Child enrolled at Smith College, her mother's alma mater, where she was sociable and physically active. Her original intent was to write the great American novel. Child graduated from Smith in 1934 with a degree in history.

Following graduation from Smith, Child lived briefly with her parents in Pasadena. In 1935 she moved to New York City, where she rented an apartment and obtained a position in a retail store as a personal shopper. Child returned to California in 1937 to help care for her mother, who had become severely ill. Caro McWilliams died later that year.

While living in California, Child worked for *Coast*, a Los Angeles–based magazine (Riley Fitch 1997), where she researched and wrote pieces on fashion. Through the Junior League she remained active in local community theater. Membership provided Child with an additional opportunity to publish, and she wrote a number of essays for the *Pasadena Junior League News* (Riley Fitch 1997).

After four years of living at home, Child moved to Washington, D.C., where she worked in the Office of Strategic Services (OSS) as part of the war effort. In 1943, after being promoted to the position of administrative assistant, Child seized upon an opportunity to work overseas and volunteered to be stationed in India. Thus, early in adulthood Child, like James Beard, set sail to explore a world far removed from her own culture.

On March 8, 1944, Child and eight other women boarded the SS *Mariposa*, a troop ship bound for India. They were the only women on board with over three thousand men. Thirty-one days later, the ship dropped anchor at Bombay. After a long train ride across India, Child reached Ceylon, where she worked in the headquarters of British general Mountbatten.

It was in Ceylon that Julia McWilliams and Paul Cushing Child first met (Riley Fitch 1997). Paul was nearly ten years older than Julia. He had traveled extensively throughout his life, beginning with his enlistment in the Canadian army at the age of sixteen. Paul had lived in Paris as a member of the expatriate society. A self-taught artist and photographer, he had been an instructor in French and art at Avon Old Farms School in Connecticut and had earned a black belt in jujitsu (Riley Fitch 1997), and Child later remarked that before she met Paul, she was simply a hayseed (Reardon 1994).

Ceylon became the site of a gastric epiphany for Julia, Paul, and their circle of friends. Together they escaped the dismal military chow offered in mess halls and plunged headlong into what Child's biographer, Noel Riley Fitch, called the curry belt. Not only did their adventures expose them to a panoply of new foods—including red, yellow, and green curries—but also to a culture far removed from twentieth-century America. Their meals were social events that frequently lasted for hours.

Less than a year after her arrival in Ceylon, Child was redeployed to the Chinese city of Kunming. Paul later joined her, and they were again transplanted to Chunking. China became another laboratory for Child's gastronomic education as her relationship with Paul deepened. As in Ceylon, Julia, Paul, and a circle of friends seized upon every opportunity to find interesting places to dine. Sanitary conditions notwithstanding, they soon learned about different regional dishes such as Szechuan and Mandarin, as well as Chinese cooking techniques. Child later described her admiration for Chinese cuisine by comparing it to the richness and complexity of French gastronomy.

As the war ground to a halt in August 1945, Julia and Paul's relationship continued to deepen. Unfortunately, Child again found herself having to endure a lengthy voyage across the Pacific Ocean. Upon returning to the United States, she rejoined her father in Pasadena and longed for her reunion with Paul.

It was while living again in Pasadena that Child made her first serious attempt to learn the craft of cooking (Reardon 1994; Riley Fitch 1997) by enrolling in cooking lessons (Riley Fitch 1997). She and a friend, Kathy Gates, traveled "three times a week to Beverly Hills for cooking classes at the Hillcliff School of Cookery, taught by Mary Hill and Irene Radcliff" (130). During this period Child purchased her first cookbook—Rombauer's 1936 edition of *The Joy of Cooking* (Reardon 1994; Riley Fitch 1997). She also acquired a number of magazines related to cooking and subsequently added more cookbooks to her collection.

Child's initial involvement with cooking had a very practical raison d'être: she wanted to please Paul and possibly to prepare for their marriage. In an interview published in *Modern Maturity* (Goodman 1994) Child described her initial involvement with food: "I didn't really start cooking until I met my husband, Paul. He had grown up with good food, so I realized I would have to learn something about it" (58).

Throughout this phase of her life, it was the desire to cook for Paul that provided Child with much of her motivation to persist in learning the craft of cooking. This perseverance helped her to cope with many failures associated with beginning cooks. For example, Child's béarnaise sauce failed because she attempted to substitute lard for butter, and a duck once caught fire in the oven because she failed to place it in a pan for roasting (Reardon 1994). As Child matured in her understanding of the craft of cooking, emotions such as passion and love probably became more pronounced. It was not just her love for Paul that was ripening. She was also falling in love with the art of cooking.

However, this passionate approach to learning cooking seems to have run contrary to the view of food preparation that was prominent in the United States during this period. In the late forties home economists—following the lead of their predecessors, the domestic scientists—continued to emphasize scientific approaches to cooking involving exact measurements and standard recipes. At the same time, food manufacturers were extolling the limitless virtues of convenience foods and gadgets, which freed the ordinary housewife from the drudgery of the kitchen. Where was there a role for passion in the process of cooking?

During this period, Child cooked for her father and friends. She kept in touch with her soul mate by mail. Paul subsequently returned to the United States and was staying with his family on the East Coast. In July 1946 he traveled to California. Reunited, he and Child drove back across the country for their planned wedding. The two were married in a civil ceremony on September 1, 1946 (Riley Fitch 1997).

Shortly after their marriage, Julia and Paul Child settled in a small home in Washington, D.C., where Paul was employed by the State Department. During this period, Child honed her cooking skills in order to please her new husband, who had discriminating tastes. The two also hosted numerous social gatherings held in their home.

Cooking for Paul and their guests provided Child with a number of opportunities to improve her culinary skills. However, cooking did not come easily to her. Paul later recalled that dinner was often served at nine or ten o'clock in the evening by an exhausted Child (Reardon 1994). Nevertheless, Child persisted in spite of her difficulties with cooking.

In 1948, when Paul was reassigned to France by the State Department, he and Child boarded the SS *America* (Riley Fitch 1997). They arrived in France five days later and, according to RIley Fitch, Child consumed a meal she would later describe as her gastronomic epiphany. This meal, which included oysters portugaises and sole meunière, has now become a part of American gastronomic folklore.

During this period of her life Child began to understand that cooking could truly be a form of art—one that could be developed and refined through dedication and hard work. It was postwar Europe, with rubble-strewn streets and continued rationing, but the Parisians still had fresh bread available three times a day (Riley Fitch 1997). The taste of French bread alone must have been an educational experience for a young woman who later wondered how American society could call itself cultured when its bread tasted like Kleenex. It was, moreover, an educational experience that she and Paul shared. This was also the time when a war-weary Elizabeth David found her voice as a food writer and captured the imagination of the English with her vivid descriptions of Mediterranean food and culture.

It was into this Parisian cosmopolitan atmosphere that Julia and Paul Child immersed themselves. According to Fitch, it was a place Child never wanted to leave (Riley Fitch 1997). She loved the vendors, restaurants, architecture, and Parisian life in general. More importantly, Child loved sharing Paris with Paul. It was in this place that Child began a lifelong love of France's grand cuisine—and perhaps also a lifelong love of learning.

In Paris Child's exposure to a world of food she had never previously encountered prompted her to enroll in a six-month course in professional cooking at the Cordon Bleu (Reardon 1994; Riley Fitch 1997). During this period, Child's typical daily routine involved attending classes in the early morning and then returning home to cook the same food for Paul later that day. Paul, family members, and visiting friends all endured such experiments with good humor. Child's rapid increase in expertise certainly did not go unnoticed by

Paul. He once compared her skills with a knife to those of the bowie knife–wielding mountain men of the American frontier.

It was in the Cordon Bleu that Child encountered her first culinary mentors, Max Bugnard and Claude Thillmont (Reardon 1994; Riley Fitch 1997). Both chefs were in the latter stages of their careers. They were supportive of Child and provided her with a sound education in the "fonds de cuisine"—the fundamentals of French cooking. It is likely that certain aspects of Child's relationship with these older men contained elements similar to that with her husband. While Paul introduced Child to a world of new foods and tastes, these instructors introduced her to the practice and theory of French cuisine. They also shared their passion for the craft with the students, as well as their connections with other members of France's gastronomical culture. In fact, it was through these instructors that Child eventually met Simone Beck and Louisette Bertholle.

It is through this interesting and invigorating web of connections that Child furthered her understanding of the principles of cooking. We do not often read or hear about the importance of relationships in learning a craft such as cooking. While writers like Michael Ruhlman talk about the importance of certain mentors in their development as cooks and chefs like Rick Bayless stress the importance of the discovery of good flavor, all too often the focus of many culinary educators is primarily on technique. When people gather to prepare and consume food, interesting social networks emerge. Whether at a picnic, a church potluck, or a clambake, food gatherings present an interesting opportunity to both celebrate and create traditions.

While Child confronted the challenges of culinary school with enthusiasm, Paul continued to be a stalwart supporter of her education. During that time he joined a men's gastronomic society and began a lifelong study of wine. He frequently shopped with Child, remaining silent when she began to acquire numerous kitchen gadgets and tools. It is difficult to overstate Paul's continued support and encouragement for Child and her cooking, all the while continuing to develop his own set of interests and skills.

Irma Rombauer and The Joy of Cooking

An American Institution

> Nevertheless, during [Julia Child's] freshman year, an event
> occurred in St. Louis that would make a major impression on her
> life. Irma Rombauer, a German American widow, and her friends
> put together a collection of recipes that they published: *The Joy
> of Cooking*.
> —Noël Riley Fitch, *Appetite for Life:
> The Biography of Julia Child*

It was the summer of 1930. The young Julia McWilliams was pursuing a degree at Smith College, while in St. Louis recently widowed Irma Rombauer began to collect recipes for a cookbook (Mendelson 1996). The initial publication of only three thousand copies was called *The Joy of Cooking: A Compilation of Reliable Recipes with a Casual Culinary Chat*. This book was significant not just for its collection of recipes but also for the informal and amiable way that Irma Rombauer welcomed people into the kitchen and explained the craft of cooking. The impact of this book and its subsequent revisions has been substantial. *The Joy of Cooking* was the only cookbook mentioned by the New York Public Library in its list of the 150 most influential books of the twentieth century (Diefendorf 1996).

Five years after the initial publication of her book, Ms. Rombauer was able to convince the publishing house Bobbs-Merrill to produce and market her cookbook. Fortunately, the editors at Bobbs-Merrill recognized the value of Ms. Rombauer's writing style, which was maintained in subsequent editions in which Rombauer was the chief contributor.

One of the important features of *The Joy of Cooking* was its accessible presentation (Finn 2000). Irma attempted to create clear, unambiguous directions, "written in a method so clear that a child can follow" (Rombauer 1936, iii). The chapters cover everything from cocktails to cakes, puddings, and desserts. She even includes a separate section on cooking in kitchenettes and provides a list of recipes suitable for cooking in close quarters: "Read this list for the lilies of the field—that toil not neither do they smell—(the latter an outstanding virtue in close quarters) and try them out" (575).

The manner in which the information was presented reflected Irma's background: she was neither a professional cook nor a writer (Wolk Salon 2002). She wrote from the standpoint of an amateur—a lover of food and cooking—for the benefit of other amateurs. Is it any wonder that her cookbook has served as a wedding present for generations of prospective cooks?

Irma Rombauer also criticized the prevailing models of cookery that existed during her era. One school of cooking promoted by domestic scientists and subsequently by home economists emphasized a scientific approach to food preparation. "Just follow my directions," barked culinary drill sergeant Fannie Farmer. Another group of cooks presented great cooking as an esoteric art, one that needed years of training to master (Wolk Salon 2002). Luckily for the rest of us cooks, Rombauer adopted a position in which the methodology of cooking was simple and straightforward and the process of cooking was promoted as a pleasurable activity.

In the fifties, Rombauer's daughter Marion added her input to *The Joy of Cooking* and assumed primary responsibility for its publication. Rombauer died in 1962, with her daughter following her in 1976. Marion's son Ethan oversaw yet another edition in 1997. Regrettably, the latest edition lacked Rombauer's distinctive voice. While *The Joy of Cooking* remains an excellent culinary reference, it has lost the personal quality. This edition reads more like a report from a focus group and not an amateur's loving description of her craft. This sentiment is echoed most aptly by Molly Finn. "Irma's voice is gone, replaced by a bland, impersonal, collective presence that lacks what was best about the old *Joy*: the unmistakable companionship of a humorous, friendly guide" (Finn 2000, 46). Fortunately, an ample supply of earlier editions of *The Joy of Cooking* is available in secondhand bookstores.

In Paris Julia and Paul Child's social circle continued to expand. In 1951 Child began to attend meetings of the Cercle des Gourmettes, a club of women dedicated to French gastronomy (Riley Fitch 1997). It was at these meetings that Child began to socialize with Simone Beck and Louisette Bertholle. She also cooked and shared recipes with them.

These three women subsequently opened a small, informal cooking school they called L'École des Trois Gourmandes. Classes, the first of which occurred in January 1952, were held in Child's kitchen. The food was produced without the benefit of a great deal of space and equipment. The cook stove was tiny. Child later described their work in the cooking school, where lessons consisted of the preparation of simple French food in a French atmosphere (Ferretti 1995).

At first classes were scheduled intermittently, with enrollment limited to five or six students. Many of the students were American friends of Child's or were sent from the American embassy. The typical class ran through the morning, with students engaged in preparation work and cooking. At noon students and instructors would eat what had been prepared in a communal-style lunch (Reardon 1994). The sharing of these meals demonstrates the importance of social relationships and the development of the craft of cooking. It might also be inferred that these events were enjoyed by everyone involved in a spirit that promoted learning. This runs contrary to the popular notion that good cooking requires a vast assortment of expensive utensils and gadgets.

The shift from student to teacher did not appear to dampen Child's readiness to continue learning. She took lessons with Max Bugnard and Claude Thillmont (Reardon 1994) and collaborated with them on a number of projects. In addition, her widening social circle provided Child with the opportunity to meet many influential members of France's food scene. Julia and Paul Child also participated in a variety of wine tastings as Paul continued his education in this field.

Child's most ambitious learning project thus far occurred in 1952, when she agreed to collaborate with Beck and Bertholle on the publication of a book devoted to French cooking and intended for the U.S. market (Reardon 1994; Riley Fitch 1997). Both women had already published a book entitled *What's Cooking in France,* but it had met with limited success in the United States (Reardon 1994). The work invested in what would eventually become the first volume of *Mastering the Art of French Cooking* spanned nearly ten years.

Child's principal task on their cookbook was to translate information into English and to create recipes that could be successfully utilized by the average amateur American cook. A major hurdle in this endeavor was adapting French recipes to ingredients available in the typical U.S. market.

The transposition of French recipes for American cooks was a staggering task. This was not simply limited to making information accessible. Indeed, Americans had developed an attitude toward food and cooking that differed from that of the French. The scientific revolution in the United States fostered the notion that all problems could be solved through scientific and technical advances—which included the challenges of food preparation. This was evident in such inventions as the TV dinner, which was popularized in the United States in the fifties. The development of this product, the result of scientific advances, was also created in response to years of advertising aimed at American housewives. These messages warned them that cooking was a drudgery (Hess and Hess 2000; Tisdale 2000) that had to be avoided at all costs. Many women regarded cooking as an unwelcome, unrewarding chore, like cleaning toilet bowls (Lehrman 1997).

The production of a book on French cooking during this period must have seemed utterly insane. After all, the United States was caught up in a scientific revolution in which anything was possible. Consumers eagerly awaited machines capable of producing small pills that resulted in savory meals served by amiable robots. Who had the time to learn how to make a good roux or a coq au vin?

In order to create a book that would appeal to Americans, Child and her colleagues had to present readers with foods that were not too complex and would be enjoyable to prepare. As Irma Rombauer had attempted more than twenty years earlier, Child and her partners needed to infuse some joy into cooking.

In addition to overcoming ingrained attitudes against cooking, the three women also had to contend with drastic differences between American supermarkets and the grocery stores in France. In the United States, for example, supermarkets promoted frozen foods and other convenience items. There was thus little or no incentive for American cooks to shop beyond the middle aisles of their supermarkets (where dried, bottled, and canned foods are shelved). As a result, supermarkets did not feel obligated to provide the variety of fresh foods available in markets such as Les Halles in Paris—foods that were considered staples by the French. Child and her coauthors also had to deal with the fact that certain products were simply unavailable to American cooks, whereas the same items could be readily purchased by the average French cook.

The production of the first volume of *Mastering the Art of French Cooking* thus required an enormous amount of research in the kitchen. Fortunately, different friends and family members were available to help. Paul, in particular, was instrumental in obtaining critical ingredients. He and Jean, Simone Beck's husband, were pressed into service as taste testers of different recipes. For example, Paul had to consume a number of different renditions of blanquette de veau on successive nights before the recipe was declared perfect.

Another important concept that had to be communicated to American cooks was how to organize their work. The concept of "mise en place"—having everything ready up to the point of preparation—may not be obvious to many American cooks, but this remains an important element of cooking. Child had probably first encountered it at the Cordon Bleu, but it was her husband who helped her to appreciate the organization of a kitchen. He applied skills he had developed while setting up war rooms for Mountbatten in India, as well as for other military leaders. An illustration of this organizational bent was Paul's use of numbered pegs upon which to hang pots, pans, and other utensils.

The Childs were reassigned yet again, this time to Germany. By 1956, however, they were bound for the United States. They returned to their home in the Georgetown neighborhood of Washington, D.C. Julia and Paul missed Paris, but this move permitted her to continue her research on the cookbook using ingredients that would be available to American readers. Child managed to maintain a high level of communication with her two collaborators despite the great distance that separated them.

In 1959 Paul's work took the Childs back to Europe. While the Childs were stationed in Oslo, Norway, Julia and her coauthors learned that the Knopf publishing house had agreed to publish their book (Reardon 1994; Riley Fitch 1997). Throughout this period Child concentrated on editorial tasks associated with preparing a final manuscript, while Paul created a set of line drawings to accompany the text. Child also continued to offer cooking lessons.

Promotion of the newly published book consumed much of their time. In fact, the Childs and Simone Beck spent a considerable amount of time promoting the cookbook at their own expense (Reardon 1994; Riley Fitch 1997). They traveled across the country to attend book signings and demonstrated their recipes. Paul was always there to provide backup support. In one situation he even had to wash dishes in a bathroom because adequate kitchen facilities were not available.

In 1962, following an interview broadcast on educational television, Child was approached and asked if she would be interested in creating three pilot television programs dedicated to cooking (Riley Fitch 1997). This was the beginning of *The French Chef* series. The pilot show, "The French Omelet," was filmed on June 18. With her engaging style and casual approach to food and cooking, Child won the hearts of television audiences. In her biography Riely Fitch describes the initial reaction of television audiences to *The French Chef*: "The great American fear of being outré and gauche was diminished by this patrician lady, who was not afraid of mistakes and did not talk down to her audience"

(293). The first program of her initial series was broadcast on January 23, 1963.

Ultimately Child taped hundreds of half-hour programs over the course of many years. According to Riely Fitch, thanks to her book and television shows Child made a significant impact on cooking during the sixties: "[S]he celebrated her appetite, the joy of the kitchen, and the pleasure of food, a pleasure conveyed in the way she patted the bread dough and caressed the chicken" (301). Child's impact was heightened by her ability to encourage the beginning cook to take chances and to not fear making mistakes.

As distribution of *The French Chef* expanded, Child's popularity surged. The show began to take on the proportions of a cult phenomenon, prompting Joan Bartel's likening of the appeal of Julia Child to such sixties phenomena as underground films and pop cults (Riley Fitch 1997).

As a result of Child's phenomenal growth in popularity, a team was put in charge of producing her television shows as well as her books. Following his retirement, Paul helped manage the production of Child's television shows, while others contributed their efforts to her publications. Simone Beck remained a close ally and friend. In fact, the Childs built a small home on the Beck property in southern France.

Child's popularity propelled her into other media. In 1967 she was featured in an article in *Ladies' Home Journal*. *Time* magazine also ran a cover story on her. The public attention showered on Child led to a formal invitation to attend a state dinner at the White House in 1967 (Riley Fitch 1997).

Despite this period of increased public attention, Child found time to collaborate with Simone Beck on the second volume of *Mastering the Art of French Cooking*. One of the features of the second volume was a recipe for French bread that could be produced in American kitchens. This single recipe reflects the amount of time Child spent learning her cooking skills. Child literally went through hundreds of pounds of flour in order to discover techniques for making a variety of French bread specialties, including baguettes (Riley Fitch 1997).

The second volume of *Mastering the Art of French Cooking* was published in the early seventies. This, together with an increase in the distribution of *The French Chef* television series, fueled Child's increasing popularity with the press and the public. She was even parodied on an episode of the television series *Saturday Night Live* in which Dan Aykroyd played Child, imitating her unique speech mannerisms while exaggeratedly dropping food on the floor and swigging wine (Riley Fitch 1997).

In the seventies Paul's health began to fail. Despite the mounting stress associated with his condition, Child maintained a heavy work schedule. She wrote *From Julia Child's Kitchen*, which was published in 1975. From 1977 to 1978 Child filmed the television series *Julia Child & Company*, which was followed by *Julia Child & More Company* from 1979 to 1980 (Riley Fitch, 1997). These series were accompanied by their respective books. In 1981 Child and a number of American food professionals founded the American Institute of Wine & Food (AIWF). The mission of this organization is stated at its Web site (Food 2001): "Founded on the premise that sharing quality food and drink is essential to the quality of human existence, The American Institute of Wine & Food is a nonprofit educational organization with membership open to all. The AIWF is dedicated to promoting the message of health and well-being through the enjoyment of good food and drink and the fellowship that comes from eating together around the table." Child was involved in both planning and fund-raising for this organization and worked with individuals such as celebrated winemaker Robert Mondavi to further its cause.

In addition to her involvement in the AIWF, Child again began teaching cooking. This included a three-year series of classes known as the "Great Chefs Series" held at the Mondavi vineyards (Riley Fitch 1997). Child's teaching included a series of six hour-long videocassettes entitled "The Way to Cook." This series later became the basis for a book of the same title that was subsequently published in 1989.

As Child's career continued to soar, she became more vocal about eating practices in the United States. She opposed the "food Nazis," who chided her for her promotion of meats and ingredients such as butter. Child also rejected fad diets and provided her own guidelines for healthy eating: eat anything you want; consume smaller portions; do not have second "helpings"; and avoid snacks.

Julia Child celebrated her eightieth birthday in 1992. To honor the occasion, a number of major culinary events were held across the United States. For example, guests in New York City paid $200 each to attend and five hundred guests in Los Angeles paid $350 apiece at the Ritz-Carlton.

In 1994 Paul Child died of coronary heart disease. Later that year Child attended a family gathering in Maine. Following the memorial service, Paul's ashes were scattered across the sea. During the years preceding Paul's death, Julia had also witnessed the deaths of Elizabeth David and M. F. K. Fisher, as well as her dear friend and colleague Simone Beck.

Child remained active in the years following Paul's death. She continued to teach, considering herself primarily an educator, cook, and food historian (Riley Fitch 1997). In the summer of 2004 she died quietly in her sleep, having attained nearly the same age as Paul.

Throughout her career Julia Child taught us about food through her work and her life. Indeed, she demonstrated how rich and interesting life can be when it includes a thoughtful appreciation for good food prepared simply and with fresh ingredients. She also stressed the importance of enjoying good food in moderation and in the company of friends.

References

American Institute of Wine & Food (AIWF). 2004. "About AIWF." Accessed October 15, 2004, at http://www.aiwf.org/site/about.html.

Child, J. 1999. "Slice of History." *People* 51: 169–78.

Coffey, R. W. 1988. "Julia and Paul Child: Their Recipe for Love." *Mc-Call's* 116: 116.

Diefendorf, E., ed. 1996. *The New York Public Library's Books of the Century.* New York: Oxford University Press.

Ferretti, F. 1995. "Julia: America's Favorite Cook." *Gourmet* 55: 70, 76.

Finn, M. 2000. "A Century in Books." *First Things* 101: 44–46.

Goodman, S. 1994. "Food for Thought." *Modern Maturity* 36: 58–63, 71.

Hess, J., and K. Hess. 2000. *The Taste of America.* Champaign: University of Illinois Press.

Lehrman, K. 1997. "What Julia Started." *U.S. News & World Report* 123: 57–61, 65.

Mendelson, A. 1996. *Stand Facing the Stove: The Story of the Women Who Gave America "The Joy of Cooking."* New York: Henry Holt.

Reardon, J. 1994. *M. F. K. Fisher, Julia Child and Alice Waters: Celebrating Pleasures of the Table.* New York: Random House.

Riley Fitch, N. 1997. *Appetite for Life: The Biography of Julia Child.* New York: Doubleday.

Rombauer, I. 1936. *The Joy of Cooking.* Indianapolis, Ind., Bobbs-Merrill.

Simpson, J. 1988. *Simpson's Contemporary Quotations: The Most Notable Quotes Since 1950.* Boston: Houghton Mifflin. Accessed October 15, 2004, at http://www.bartleby.com/63/84/6384.html.

Tisdale, S. 2000. *The Best Thing I Ever Tasted: The Secret of Food.* New York: Penguin, Putnam.

Wolk Salon, D. 2002. "The Joy of 'Joy': Timeless Classic Embraces the Pleasure of Cooking." *Chicago Sun Times* July 17.

Elizabeth David

Writing Sensually about Food and Culture

Provence is a country to which I am always returning,
next week, next year, any day now, as soon as I can get
onto a train. Here in London it is an effort of will to believe
in the existence of such a place at all. But now and again
the vision of golden tiles on a round southern roof, or of
some warm, stony, herb-scented hillside will
rise out of my kitchen pots with the smell of a piece
of orange peel scenting a beef stew.
—Elizabeth David, in *South Wind through the Kitchen:*
The Best of Elizabeth David

ARISTOCRATIC, SENSUAL and at times enigmatic, Elizabeth
David wrote forcefully about food for over four decades. The passionate and sensual style of this writer is reflected in the introduction
to her first book, *A Book of Mediterranean Food* (David 1950), where
she writes: "The cooking of the Mediterranean shores, endowed
with all the natural resources, the color and flavor of the south, is
a blend of tradition and brilliant improvisation. The Latin genius
flashes from the kitchen pans" (5). For David, writing about food
also involved writing about people and places: the splendor of market stalls; the aromatic fragrances of dried herbs; heaps of fresh fish;
and pungent local wines.

Writing such as this influenced countless cooks around the globe.

It was against the backdrop of postwar food rationing that Elizabeth David wrote *Mediterranean Food*. In it she captured the imaginations and hearts of English cooks, holding them captive with her subsequent publications. In fact, Jill Norman (1993), David's publisher and friend, once described the magnitude of David's impact on an entire generation of English cooks: "In the sixties many an enthusiastic amateur opened a small restaurant with little more than his or her well-used copies of Elizabeth David, the necessary minimum of equipment and the will to succeed. And many of them did" (35).

The lifelong journey that carried Elizabeth David, née Gwynne, from the English countryside to writing at the kitchen table began with her birth on December 26, 1913. She and her three sisters—Priscilla, Diana, and Felicite—grew up in relative comfort. Their maternal grandfather was a conservative member of Parliament who was later named home secretary (Chaney 1998; Cooper 1999). James Gwynne, their paternal grandfather, was a successful industrialist who owned a considerable amount of property, including an estate, Folkington Manor, and an attractive house in Wootton (Chaney 1998). It was in the manor house that Rupert and Stella Gwynne settled following James Gwynne's death. Rupert, a barrister and a member of Parliament, and Stella jointly managed the home.

David's parents did not hold much interest in cooking or the kitchen. They had no need to know anything about cookery since this was the responsibility of their domestic staff. Lisa Chaney (1998) has described Stella's attitude toward cooking as follows: "In keeping with most well-off women at the turn of the century Stella was not interested in the kitchens, and she seldom entered them" (19). Chaney also relates that the Gwynne children were not encouraged to visit the kitchen: "Here [in the Wootton kitchen] the girls were not welcomed. Nor were they recompensed by delicious foods pulled up to their nursery and schoolroom from the kitchen down below. With few exceptions, these meals were of little cheer" (20).

This atmosphere was far removed from the Beard household, where little James was free to waddle in and out of the kitchen at will.

The lack of interest in food and cooking on the part of the Gwynnes arose, in part, from the ingrained attitudes of the era. Children were often forbidden to enjoy rich food and drink because they were viewed as impeding the development of moral fiber. In fact, the mere discussion of food and drink was prohibited by custom. According to Chaney (1998), at the end of the nineteenth century a proper Englishman considered any discussion of the pleasures of the table to be vulgar, evidence of the medieval sin of gluttony. Since the Gwynne family expected their daughters to marry into families of substance, there was little or no need for them to be knowledgeable about cooking or other tasks normally assigned to the domestic staff. Given this background, it is hard to conceive of David writing about sweets purchased in a pastry shop in Toulouse just a few years later. "[A]s I walked away carrying my pretty little tin of childish sweets I thought how often some such trivial little discovery colors and alters in one's mind the whole aspect of a city or countryside" (51). Sensuous writing such as this captured the imagination of many of her readers.

The relative comfort of the Gwynne sisters was derailed in 1923 when their father died. Their grandfather had established a will that specified transfer of property to male members of the family. This left Rupert's brother in charge of the Gwynne family estates. Although Stella and her daughters were permitted to remain in the family home, their financial condition became tenuous.

Following her father's death, David spent several years in a boarding school, Godstowe Preparatory School (Chaney 1998). At the age of sixteen David was sent by her mother to board with two other English girls in Paris, where all three attended classes at the Sorbonne.

David's stay in Paris marked the beginning of a long love affair with food and cooking. These early experiences undoubtedly helped to inspire a unique personal style of writing about food that was far removed from the science-based recipes of home economists or those who held an assembly-line attitude toward cooking and eating. After all, David's writing career was launched during the same era that witnessed the birth and exponential growth of fast food.

The sentimental streak inherent in David's writing can be appreciated in the following description of a Norman market (David 1952): "Delicate rose pink langoustines lie next to miniature scallops in their red-brown shells; great fierce skate and sleek soles are flanked by striped iridescent mackerel, pearly little smelts, and baskets of very small, very black little mussels" (25). It is not simply the romantic style of David's writing that appeals to our culinary hearts and souls. She, like James Beard, validates the importance and sensuality associated with all aspects of cooking, including shopping for fresh produce at the market.

While in Paris, David and the other young women boarded with a French family, the Barettes. Unfortunately, David found her surroundings quite stifling (Cooper 1999). Nevertheless, she later noted (David 1952) that this was the time when she first learned to appreciate French food, adding that every member of the family seemed to be "food-conscious" (28). Even though the Barettes did not spend a great deal of money on groceries, their food was delicious despite its simplicity.

It was in these circumstances that David had an opportunity to observe the work of the family cook, Léontine. She also had time to develop an appreciation for Madame Barette's dedication to shopping for food at Les Halles (David 1952). This matronly woman spent a considerable amount of time and energy several days each week at this market. She would return loaded down with large bags of food for the family. This dedication to family nourishment was far more personal than what David had been accustomed to in her own home.

Toward the end of David's eighteen-month residence in France, she had an opportunity to stay with the Barettes at their country home in Normandy. During this period Léontine was on holiday, and it was then that David ate food prepared by a young French-woman who replaced Léontine. This woman was nearly the same age as David. On one occasion she prepared a dish of mussels for David, who had never eaten shellfish. Later in life she recalled the experience: "So those Norman mussels, which reminded me, for whatever reason, of our secret childhood feasts [wild mushrooms in cream sauce cooked by their nanny], became forever endowed with the mystery of far off and almost unobtainable things" (Cooper 1999, 31).

Following her stay in France, David lived in Munich, where she studied German. She returned to England for her eighteenth birthday and her coming out party. As a young debutante David radiated physical beauty and charm. Having spent a considerable amount of time on the Continent, she was fluent in three languages. At the age of twenty she left home to join the Oxford Repertory Company as an assistant stage manager, hoping to become an actress someday.

David worked for the company until 1934, when she joined the Open Air Theater in Regent's Park (Cooper 1999). It was during this time that David met Leonard (Charles) Gibson Cowan, an actor/writer in his late twenties. Her relationship with Cowan would later take David on an epic journey that would shape the rest of her life.

Despite the fact that the salary David earned from her work in the theater was supplemented by her family, she constantly struggled to pay her bills. Armed with several cookbooks, and in a style reminiscent of the young James Beard or Eugene Walter, David began to cook for herself as a way to make ends meet. In one cookbook in particular, *The Gentle Art of Cookery* (Leyel and Hartley 1929), David found both information and inspiration.

David outfitted the landing outside her room as a kitchen, where she cooked for herself and for members of the theater company. Among her frequent guests was Charles Cowan. Despite the fact that he was married, their relationship deepened, much to the disapproval of David's family.

As a way to separate her from Charles, David's mother encouraged her to travel. Accordingly, in 1936 David visited her sister Priscilla and her husband, Richard Longland, on the island of Malta, where they lived. While there, she observed their cook, Angela, who exuded a passion for food and cooking (Cooper 1999). As with the young Frenchwoman who, while standing in for Léontine, served up the feast of Normal mussels, Angela demonstrated a truly personal approach to cooking. For these two individuals, cooking represented far more than a set of mechanical tasks. In addition to being a source of pride, cooking for these women confirmed their personal identity and uniqueness.

While on this trip, David also visited Cairo and the Levant—specifically Palestine, Lebanon, and Syria. The trip, lasting nearly five months, opened David's eyes to new foods and cultures. Her understanding of and affinity for the craft of cooking was gradually developing.

Returning to London, David was unable to secure satisfactory employment. She renewed her relationship with Charles Cowan. Together they decided to purchase a boat in order to cruise the Mediterranean (Cowan 1946). Fortified with funds from her uncle Jasper, early in 1938 Elizabeth and Charles purchased a two-masted yawl, the *Evelyn Hope* (Cooper 1999). The boat was in disrepair and required a large investment of money and time. Finally, in July 1939 Elizabeth, Charles, and another passenger set sail from Southampton as the clouds of war began to sweep across the European landscape. At about this time M. F. K. Fisher was making plans to return to the United States with her ailing husband.

The images evoked by life aboard a sailboat are often romantic. It is all too easy to focus on the boat's graceful passage through gently rising swells, a deep azure sky, and the fragrance of saltwater wafted on a gentle breeze. With Charles at the wheel, a glass of wine in one hand, could there be a more perfect setting for preparing and enjoying good food and conversation?

The fact of the matter was that conditions on the *Evelyn Hope* were severe, providing David with a serious challenge to her newly developed cooking skills. Storage on the boat was restricted and primitive. A limited amount of refrigeration would have reduced the availability of fresh produce and meat. Likewise, cooking was restricted to a Primus stove, which is similar to a small, portable camp stove. In an era that includes microwave ovens, blenders, freeze-dried food, vacuum-seal packaging, and a vast array of convenience foods, one tends to underestimate the limited cooking options available to Elizabeth and Charles.

The unsteady movement of a small craft compounded problems associated with limited equipment and provisions. Nearly sixty years after the voyage of the *Evelyn Hope*, Diana Jesse (1997) has some pithy advice for would-be galley cooks on yachts: "Items in the galley need to be easily reached, particularly if you are wearing a safety harness" (33). Steve Colgate (1996) adds that a cook should brace against the bulkhead in order have both hands free to prepare food. Given the conditions of a small boat at sea, it is conceivable that tasks as simple as making coffee would have been highly complicated. Colgate hints at this when he recommends procedures for pouring coffee into a cup. He says that one person should hold both the cup and the coffeepot. If two people attempt the task, it is too difficult to coordinate the pot with the cup while maintaining one's balance. All too frequently scalding liquid will burn one or both people.

A further complication of Elizabeth and Charles's situation involved a lack of funds. In order to afford the journey, they were forced to take on a paying guest, who traveled with them to France and abruptly returned to England as fears of war on the Continent worsened. At the time of the outbreak of hostilities between France and Germany, Elizabeth and Charles were situated in a small port in the south of France (Cowan 1946). Despite the impending conflagration, Elizabeth and Charles continued their trek through the Mediterranean.

It was in France that David met the writer Norman Douglas (Chaney 1998). The latter had written extensively about food and eating, in particular Mediterranean culture and its cuisine. David's relationship with Douglas was to have a lasting impact on her writing. This influence is reflected in the title of her collected writings, *South Wind through the Kitchen* (Norman 1998), which was named, in part, after Douglas's opus *South Wind*.

On a number of occasions David emphasized the influence Douglas had on her life, once even expressing her love for the man. She later wrote two essays about their relationship (Cooper 1999). M. M. Pack (2001) once described the relationship between the seventy-two-year-old writer and the twenty-six-year-old David. Douglas was well versed in food and dining. He taught the young David how to eat well and fostered her appreciation for the best that life had to offer. Douglas spoke openly about the joys of food at a time when such talk was considered impolite. For him food mattered because it was a fundamental aspect of life and consequently should be enjoyed to the fullest (Cooper 1999).

Douglas's attitudes toward food echo throughout David's writings, and she even dedicated her first book to his memory. Douglas not only provided her with information about food but challenged her, through his example, to engage in rigorous scholarship, to seek out the true and authentic, in addition to striving for excellence in matters of food and wine (Chaney 1998). This latter influence was evident in the scholarship reflected in her writing, in which she frequently referred to Douglas's publications.

Douglas asked David to leave Charles and remain with him on the Continent. David later suggested that although she might have been better off had she remained with Douglas, she would have missed out on the experiences that contributed to her development as a cookery writer. David chose to sail away with Charles, and both were subsequently swept up in the maelstrom of World War II. It was not until long after Douglas's death that David (1952) talked about him and how he had touched her life:

> A more fitting place to remember [Douglas] was in the lemon grove
> to be reached only by descending some three hundred steps from

the Piazza. It was so thick, that lemon grove, that it concealed from all but those who knew their Capri well the archbishops' palace in which was housed yet another of those private taverns which appeared to materialize for Norman alone. There, at a table outside the half-ruined house, a branch of piercingly aromatic lemons hanging within arm's reach, a piece of bread and a bottle of the proprietor's olive oil in front of me, a glass of wine in my hand, Norman was speaking. (125)

Elizabeth and Charles's journey became more problematic when Italy declared war against the Allies. On the day Italy entered the war, while attempting to pass through the straits of Messina, their boat was captured by the Italians (Chaney 1998; Cooper 1999). They were held briefly by Italian authorities, who thought they might be spies. The *Evelyn Hope* was never returned, leaving them stranded in Italy without funds. With the assistance of the American consulate, they were able to flee to Athens. Charles obtained a teaching position in the Greek islands, where they lived for a time on the island of Syros (Chaney 1998; Cooper 1999).

According to Artemis Cooper (1999; 2000), conditions on Syros were primitive. Their water was obtained from a well and most cooking was accomplished outdoors on a small brazier. Their bathroom consisted of a small hut with a hole in the ground (Cowan 1946); Charles later recalled that when David saw their "outhouse," she joked about the nonexistent marble floor and the fact that at least it had a roof.

The tools and products we take for granted nowadays were simply not available on Syros. David did not have refrigeration or other appliances. David was reduced to a limited selection of foods with which she could cook. There were no supermarkets containing canned, frozen, and prepared foods. Their diet consisted primarily of foods from the local open-air market and what could be harvested from the sea, primarily fish and octopus, which David continued to love throughout her life.

Elizabeth and Charles remained on Syros until Germany invaded Yugoslavia and Greece. As the German invasion progressed, Syros was bombed and the couple fled to Cyprus in a small boat. After the Germans attacked Cyprus, they were evacuated and finally made their way to Egypt. It was in Cairo that they parted company.

In Egypt David found work as a civil servant with the British government. She moved to Alexandria and immediately immersed herself in this multicultural city populated by Turks, Arabs, Jews, Copts, Italians, Armenians, Greeks, Syrians, Americans, and the British (Cooper 1999). Later David was transferred to Cairo, where she remained for the duration of the war.

David's subsequent employment in Egypt exposed her to the foods of a cosmopolitan, international community. She also had the financial resources to hire a series of cooks, one of whom, Kyriacou, taught her about foods available in the marketplace and demonstrated how good food could be prepared under relatively primitive conditions. For example, much of the cooking had to be accomplished using a Primus stove similar to the one David had used on the *Evelyn Hope*.

However, Kyriacou provided David with more than just knowledge about cooking. Like Douglas, he exuded a passion for the craft. This is reflected in David's description of an octopus dinner Kyriacou prepared to celebrate the fact that his family had escaped the war (Cooper 1999). In a deep pot he built a bed of thyme branches on which he placed layers of "onions, tomatoes, garlic, bay leaves and olives, and then the octopus. Gently he poured red wine over his carefully constructed edifice, stirred in the ink from the fish, and left his covered pot to simmer for the rest of the afternoon" (87).

David was later assisted by another cook named Suleiman, who deepened her understanding of Mediterranean food (Cooper 1999). David regularly hosted lunches in her apartment, where she could share her passion for food with friends and colleagues. She and Suleiman collaborated in these events. According to Artemis Cooper (1999), the preparation of these meals still posed quite a challenge:

"The lunches, as Elizabeth was the first to acknowledge, were a joint effort between her and Suleiman, on fairly primitive equipment. They had a portable charcoal grill and two Primus stoves, while a square tin box perched on one of the stoves served as an oven" (104). Like his predecessor, Suleiman conveyed a sense of cooking as a special activity. David later described Suleiman's "lavish hand with herbs and seasonings" and spoke of his "devoted watch" (104) over the cooking.

In Cairo David met and subsequently married Tony David, a British officer of Indian descent. Elizabeth's marriage to Tony took her to India. This was not a culture whose cuisine had captivated the likes of Julia McWilliams and Paul Child. However, later in life David did write knowledgeably about curries, due, at least in part, to her brief stay in India. Cooper (1999) nevertheless has stated that she loathed British India.

According to Artemis Cooper (1999), after the war Elizabeth David returned to an England that continued to be gripped by food shortages and rationing. David refused to be limited by the rationing. She viewed conditions as a challenge, later recalling that "with whatever I could get, I cooked as one possessed" (127). David compared the conditions to those she had experienced in Egypt. She noted that even though the standard of living in Egypt had not been very high, the food she was able to procure had "life" to it—there were always interesting smells and flavors. From these words we can see how David's relationship with food and cooking had changed over the years.

It was in the midst of the austerity brought about by continued postwar rationing and shortages that Elizabeth began to write about Mediterranean food. According to Cooper (1999), the original impetus was her longing for the sunny skies of the Levant. She also based her future book on over twelve years of cooking performed under difficult conditions, with minimal equipment. These experiences not only helped David develop a useful set of cooking skills but also enabled her to acquire a sophisticated sense of taste that

Chaney (1998) has described as "at once fastidious, traditional, catholic and bohemian" (210).

The result of David's work was a book entitled *A Book of Mediterranean Food* (1950). In addition to providing authentic recipes that were not altered to accommodate the restrictions of rationing,, the book also described the life of the people of the region as a context for their food. David wanted to bring the foods alive for a nation that had experienced years of deprivation.

It is interesting to note that David's original manuscript for *A Book of Mediterranean Food* was returned by her publisher, who claimed it needed more information about the foods contained in the recipes. This was due, in part, to David's misguided notion that she did not have anything of substance to contribute and that she needed to keep her voice out of the book and focus on the recipes. Fortunately, her publisher disagreed and insisted that she provide more than a conglomeration of recipes (Cooper 1999).

In order to add depth to *A Book of Mediterranean Food,* David consulted writers such as Henry James, Marcel Boulestin, Robert Byron, and D. H. Lawrence (Cooper 1999) for her descriptions of the people of the Mediterranean. The information provided by these writers, however, was not sufficient. David also had to rely on her own experience and learn to speak with her own voice. What emerged were passages such as her description of a fisherman who prepared the shellfish he had just caught for her. It is also evident in her introduction to *A Book of Mediterranean Food* (David 1950): "The cooking of the Mediterranean shores, endowed with all the natural resources, the color and flavor of the South, is a blend of tradition and brilliant improvisation. The Latin genius flashes from the kitchen pans" (5). Could these be the words of the same woman who, a few years earlier, did not know how to brew tea?

David continued to write books and magazine articles throughout the remainder of her life. In the sixties she embarked on a business venture and opened a cookware store in London. Even though the ownership of a retail cookware store may not, at first blush, appear to be a source of learning for a woman who had previously written extensively about food and cooking, David was compelled to engage in a considerable amount of travel and research in order to obtain products for her customers.

David left behind a rich legacy for cooks and food lovers on several continents. While stressing the need to know the basics of cooking, David also focused on the preservation of cultural traditions associated with food, promoting the pleasures of both cooking and eating. For this we will always be in her debt.

References

Chaney, L. 1998. *Elizabeth David*. London: Macmillan.

Colgate, S. 1996. *Fundamentals of Sailing, Cruising and Racing*. New York: Norton.

Cooper, A. 1999. *Writing at the Kitchen Table: The Authorized Biography of Elizabeth David*. New York: HarperCollins.

———. 2000. Elizabeth, A Rebel in the Kitchen. *The Times* (London) November 18: 16.

Cowan, G. 1946. *The Voyage of the "Evelyn Hope."* London: Cresset Press.

David, E. 1950. *A Book of Mediterranean Food*. London: John Lehman.

———. 1952. *An Omelette and a Glass of Wine*. New York: Lyons Press.

———, ed. 1980. *Elizabeth David Classics*. Newton, Mass.: Biscuit Books.

Jesse, D. 1997. *The Cruising Woman's Advisor: How to Prepare for the Voyaging Life*. Camden, Maine: International Marine.

Leyel, C., and O. Hartley. 1929. *The Gentle Art of Cookery*. London: Chatto & Windus.

Norman, J. 1993. Elizabeth David. In *Out of the Frying Pan: Seven Women Who Changed the Course of Postwar Cookery*, ed. H. Castell and K. Griffin. London: BBC Books.

———, ed. 1998. *South Wind through the Kitchen: The Best of Elizabeth David*. New York: North Point Press.

Pack, M. M. 2001. "Writing at the Kitchen Table: The Authorized Biography of Elizabeth David." *Austin Chronicle*, February 16. Accessed at http://www.austinchronicle.com/issues/dispatch/2001–02–16/food_mini.html.

Mama Dip

A Lifetime of Cooking

> I was called "Dip" by my brothers and sisters from an early
> age because I was so tall (today, I am six feet, one inch)
> and had such long arms that I could reach way down in
> the rain barrel to scoop up a big dipperful of water when
> the level was low. Filling up water buckets for the kitchen
> had its benefits, though, as it was on my trips in and out
> of the kitchen with water that I first learned how to cook,
> watching how Roland or my older sisters made things with
> their "dump cooking" methods and making mental notes
> about how ingredients went together.
> —Mildred Council, *Mama Dip's Kitchen*

GIVEN THAT THE Culinary Institute of America (CIA) gradu-
ates a class every few weeks, it is not difficult to envision phalanxes
of aspiring chefs entering the hospitality industry. Over the years,
their numbers have swelled, in part in reaction to the evolution of
the occupation of chef from blue-collar worker to professional and
even celebrity.

The academic pathway for these promising careers is now called
the culinary arts, with a variety of private and public academic institutions offering excellent training in this field. Graduation from
schools such as the CIA, the New England Culinary Institute
(NECI), or Johnson and Wales University is a source of pride for

individuals as well as their families. However, it is important to also acknowledge those good cooks who learn and express their craft through a sense of love and commitment to others, especially their families. It was in the context of her interest in cooking as well as her dedication to others that Mildred Council (aka Mama Dip) wrote *Mama Dip's Kitchen* (Council 1999), which also introduced readers to her interesting life.

Mildred Council, the youngest of seven children, was raised in rural North Carolina. Her mother, Effie Edwards Cotton, was college-educated and taught in a local one-room schoolhouse. Her father, Ed, was a sharecropper. Mildred was less than two years old when Effie died, leaving Ed to raise the children as a single parent. (He never remarried.)

In spite of the family's meager income, Council claimed that she never felt poor. Like the Campbell family of Angus Campbell on Lewis Island, the Cottons were close to the land and the seasons. They enjoyed the arrival of fresh strawberries, blackberries, and asparagus in the spring. If they were lucky, fresh corn came in early July. In the fall they foraged in the woods for muscadine grapes and harvested field peas, apples, and corn. In the winter it was time to butcher the hogs, making sure to use every part of the animal. The family also bred cows and churned their milk for butter. They raised chickens, with dominickers, Rhode Island Reds, and leghorns each producing a different type of egg. Lastly, they hunted and fished the local rivers.

The Cotton family thrived on whatever was available for the table. In a voice similar to that of John Thorne, Council described the satisfaction of enjoying what was available: "When food was short, we had fun just seeing each other spread food all over the plate so it looked like a lot and counting how many biscuits each of us ate. If the butter gave out before it got to you, you had to sop your biscuits with side meat or put shoulder grease in your molasses and sop your biscuits with that" (1999, 12)

It was within this close-knit family that Council began to cook.

She did so at the bequest of her father, who one day asked her to stay at home and "fix something to eat" while the rest of the family was leaving to work in the field. For Council the opportunity to cook for her family was exciting. She spoke of the different meals they ate each day: a hearty breakfast, a main meal at midday, and a light dinner. The technique she learned and applied was called dump cooking, which had been part of the heritage of black American women. As she explained, "Dump cooking means no recipes, just measure by eye and feel and taste and testing." Council also stated that "measuring cups were not found in our kitchen" (4).

As she matured, Council continued to perfect her knowledge of dump cooking. She and her siblings also benefited from participating in a supportive community. For example, several Sundays a month during the warmer seasons the family would visit a favorite aunt and uncle who were childless and consequently loved the children as though they were "their own."

The Cotton children all attended school. The family decided to move when the one-room schoolhouse was closed. Council subsequently attended a local high school. When wartime price controls made life on their small farm impossible, "Papa" Cotton was forced to move into the town of Chapel Hill (Univ. of North Carolina Press 2004). Council was brokenhearted. At the recommendation of her family, she attended beauty school, where she met Joe, her future husband.

After her marriage, Council worked as a cook in a dormitory at the University of North Carolina. She also worked as a short-order cook in a local diner. By 1949 she had given birth to seven children. Council continued to cook while she raised her children and later joined her mother-in-law in a small catering business to "sharpen" her entrepreneurial skills.

In 1976 Council was offered the opportunity to "take over a failing restaurant" owned by a local real estate broker. She and her family took over the restaurant on a Saturday evening and worked into the night cleaning it up. The next day Council spent $64—most of her available cash—to purchase food for breakfast service. Fortunately, none of her initial customers needed change, and she used the money earned from breakfast to purchase food for lunch and dinner. That first day the restaurant netted Mildred $135. As she later wrote, "I was in business! I named my restaurant Dip's Country Kitchen." The name was later changed to Dip's as a result of a copyright issue. As the restaurant grew in popularity, Council was able to employ many family members to help manage the operation. The lessons her children learned from this experience included an appreciation for fresh food and trusting one's senses. Council also taught her children the value of hard work. As her own father had taught her, Council encouraged them to be strong.

With the success of Mama Dip's restaurant came publicity. At times this increased attention added to the challenges of operating the restaurant. For example, Council and her family once learned that the magazine *Southern Living* was planning to write an article about the restaurant to appear in the May issue. That month, as was her custom, Council permitted many on her staff to take time off to enjoy the Memorial Day weekend—without realizing that the May issue had already appeared.

On Saturday morning of the long weekend, Council and some of her staff arrived at the restaurant, where a line of eager customers extended around the corner. Council drafted all available family members and staff into service. They soon ran out of food and were forced to make repeated trips to the grocery store throughout the day. The pace did not slow down until closing time Sunday evening. The experience taught family members, such as Mildred's daughter Spring, a lesson about the value of hard work—as well as the importance of crowd control.

In the ensuing years, Mama Dip's restaurant has become a Chapel Hill institution, attracting clientele from all walks of life, including *New York Times* food critic Craig Claiborne and basketball star/restauranteur Michael Jordan. Mama Dip has been featured on *Good Morning America* as well as the Food Network's *Cooking Live* (The Original Mama Dip's 2004).

John Thorne

The Beauty of Simple Food

It's my experience that truly good cooks are born. I was not born to be one, and I don't like being trained, especially if the result is going to be mere competency. I've generally found life a lot more interesting learning to use my limitations than struggling to overcome them.
—John Thorne, *Outlaw Cook*

John Thorne, like other members of his generation who were born during the war years (Ruhlman 2005), was raised by his mother while the family waited for his father to return from military service (Thorne and Thorne 2000). His father eventually came home but decided to remain in the army in order to pursue a military career. As with other dependents of career military personnel, Thorne and his family moved around on numerous occasions. With each move came different housing accommodations, none of which provided him with that sense of home he had experienced while living with his grandparents.

When Thorne wished to express a sense of place, he frequently referred to his grandparents' summer cottage, "built at the edge of a cliff on an island in Casco Bay, Maine" (Thorne and Thorne 2000, 5). This rustic dwelling, habitable only in summer, was a place "made tangible to the senses" (7). It was a place to dig clams, pick berries, and roast hot dogs over campfire coals on the beach. The summer cottage was also a place to slow down. In fact, Thorne entitled a chapter of his book *Outlaw Cook* (Thorne 1994) "The Discovery of Slowness." This was also a place where Thorne, like Mildred Council, came to appreciate the excellence of simple foods harvested locally and consumed in season. For Thorne life at the cottage represented more than just the pleasures associated with simple, good food. It was there that he was given an opportunity to cook in the kitchen with his grandmother. These memories include helping assemble the ingredients for summer desserts utilizing locally grown blueberries, such as blueberry bread-and-butter pudding, a family favorite (Thorne and Thorne 2000).

Armed with this wealth of experiences but few physical resources, Thorne set himself up in a small apartment in New York City. Even as a young man he was determined to become a writer. It would probably be an understatement to say that Thorne's lifestyle was spartan. His furnishings included a table missing several legs and a cast iron frying pan that was the centerpiece of his food-preparation equipment. Working as a mail clerk for fifty dollars a week did not provide him with much discretionary income.

Despite admitting to being a "picky eater," the young man made periodic forays into the neighborhoods that surrounded his apartment building. He visited Little Italy and Chinatown. His history as a picky eater coupled with a sense of shyness held him back from experimenting. He became a gastronomic voyeur, peering into display cases and shop windows and hovering around vendors' stalls at markets.

Like Rick Bayless and John T. Edge, Thorne soon discovered the pleasures of street food. He later wrote about the enjoyment associated with eating empanadas cooked in hot oil at a small stand created out of a wooden packing crate. The reader can almost visualize the steam escaping from the hot pocket of dough as Thorne consumes one empanada after another on a cold winter's night following a double feature.

In this essay we can glimpse this self-described picky eater beginning to experiment. Here Thorne also reveals another aspect of his personality, namely, his strong sense of curiosity. The reader finds Thorne at his best: questioning his basic assumptions and experiences with food.

Like many struggling writers, such as Eugene Walter, Thorne was prevented from dining out regularly due to his limited income. Of necessity, he soon learned how to make do with simple foods and, like Mildred Council and her siblings, to appreciate what little food he had on his plate. It was during this period that Thorne began to cook. This was dispatched in a perfunctory manner, like brushing his teeth, and was not yet what he later described as a part of himself (Thorne 1994).

Thorne's first culinary creation was prompted by a custom he had developed. Every payday Thorne would purchase a day-old loaf of challah and a slab of butter. Upon returning to his apartment, he would tear off chunks of bread and wrap them around slices of butter, with the last mouthful consisting of a pat of butter used to pick up the remaining bits of crust that had fallen onto the table. One is reminded of M. F. K. Fisher warming segments of tangerine on a steam heater.

As Thorne analyzes the various components of this experience in a manner similar to his literal tearing apart of the loaf of bread, he displays a willingness to share his most intimate thoughts with the reader. He also makes us aware of the simplest eating experiences and their importance in our lives.

For example, in describing a plowman's lunch Thorne assumes the task of describing an interesting way to enjoy cheese and crackers (Thorne 1994). Take a cracker. Daub it with a little mustard. Add a bit of sharp New York cheddar cheese and thinly sliced pickled onion. Wash this down with a swig of ale. Forget haute cuisine. This is an earthy and readily accessible way to enjoy food.

Even though Thorne left New York City behind for a traditional college education and a teaching career, he later combined his early experiences with his endless sense of curiosity, resulting in a newsletter he entitled *Simple Food*. Devoting his full energies to writing, Thorne subsequently collaborated with his wife, Matt Lewis Thorne, to write several books, one of which, *Pot on the Fire*, won the 2001 James Beard Award (Reilly 2001).

One of the greatest lessons provided by such writers as John Thorne and John T. Edge is the need to take chances in the kitchen and at the table. For Thorne one way to learn how to cook is to master simple dishes such as fried eggs. The novice needs just a little encouragement to take this simple dish and alter it with any available modifiers in the "refrigerator/thesaurus" (Thorne 1994). Whether these "modifiers" consist of a simple pat of butter, onion garlic, sweet or hot peppers, or just a dash of a favorite condiment, the cook begins to "own" his or her creation. Cooking thus goes beyond the routine associated with tasks such as brushing one's teeth.

In addition to his encouragement of experimentation, Thorne also provides readers with an opportunity to appreciate traditions associated with such foods as baked beans (Carter 1996). However, he does not simply preach about tradition but is always willing to show how traditional dishes can be tweaked and adjusted to suit the cook's individual tastes or accommodate interesting ingredients that might be at hand. The result is an opportunity for readers to both consider new foods and think of traditional foods in new ways (Brockman 2000).

The rhythm and depth of Thorne's writing evokes a response that could be equated with a meditation on subjects as simple as baked beans, fried potatoes, and marketplaces. Thorne's in-depth understanding of his subject is evident in his ability to cite a broad range of literature directly or tangentially related to the topic under discussion. My response to Thorne's writing is to want to curl up with one of his essays and then plan an entire day dedicated to preparing a few dishes very slowly.

In addition to offering a wide range of recipes, her cookbook is also part memoir, reflecting the thoughts of a woman who has worked to make a positive impact on her world (Univ. of North Carolina Press 2004).

Perhaps one of Council's greatest gifts has been to instill in her children and grandchildren a sense of pride for hard work, reflecting the virtues of pride and self-reliance taught by Martin Luther King Jr. (Guy 1998). Through her writing and storytelling Council has also shown how local traditions and family memories are an important part of life. Through her cooking, she and others like her have provided comfort to others. The cooking that Council promotes, moreover, is simple and straightforward, based on fresh ingredients and a reliance on the senses. Council encourages us to adopt a practical approach to cooking—and a heartfelt manner in relating to others though food.

In the introduction to her book Council relates a story about a time when she planted a pumpkin seed. She tended it throughout the summer, and it produced two pumpkins. The larger pumpkin was used to create a jack-o'-lantern, and the smaller was transformed into pies and breads that Council shared with neighbors, particularly "the sick and shut-ins" (Council 1999, xi). Some of the remaining seeds provided food for wild birds. This story sheds light on the life of a woman who has dedicated herself to nurturing many people by establishing a small, independent restaurant. In addition to serving meals to thousands of visitors who have come to her restaurant, Council has simultaneously nurtured her family and promoted the well-being of her community.

References

Brockman, T. 2000. "Digging into a Helping of the Most Delicious Food Books of the Year." In *Food for Thought: Come and Get It.* Accessed February 9, 2005, at http://www.bookmagazine.com/issue13/foodfor-thought.shtml.

Carter, S. 1996. "Food for the Soul." *Newsday* December 15.

Council, M. 1999. *Mama Dip's Kitchen.* Chapel Hill: University of North Carolina Press.

Guy, A. J. 1998. "Mama Dip." *News & Observer* (Chapel Hill, N.C.) April 19.

The Original Mama Dip's. 2004. Accessed on December 29, at http://www.mamadips.com.

Reilly, E. C. 2001. "Food Industry's Oscars: The Beard Awards." *Newsday* May 2.

Ruhlman, M. "Michael Ruhlman." 2005. Accessed on March 7, at http://www.ruhlman.com.

Thorne, J. 1994. *Outlaw Cook.* New York: North Point Press.

————, and M. Lewis Thorne. 2000. *Serious Pig: An American Cook in Search of His Roots.* New York: North Point Press.

University of North Carolina Press. 2004. "Recipe for Brunswick Stew." Accessed on December 29, at http://www.uncpress.unc.edu/books/t-1522.html.

Eugene Walter

A Troubadour from the Kitchen

Gumbo born and gumbo bred,
Tabasco follies fuzz my head.
South is my blood and South my bone
So haply formed on pork and pone.
Incan, African move in me.
You say: "South, where can it be?"
Chewing my sugar cane, I repeat:
"Why, in all we cook and eat."
—Eugene Walter,
American Cooking: Southern Style

AT ABOUT THE SAME TIME that Julia McWilliams and Paul Child were exploring the culinary underbelly of southern Asia in order to escape the blandness of mess hall food, a Southern boy from Mobile, Alabama, named Eugene Walter was digging for oysters in the Arctic beaches of an Aleutian island off the coast of Alaska. The Aleutians hardly constitute a source of culinary inspiration. Eugene Walter's quest in that frigid region was to find ingredients for a make-shift gumbo that he wished to share with his comrades. He, too, was attempting to find relief from the nondescript chow served up in army mess halls. Creating special foods and memorable moments became a lifelong goal in Eugene Walter's life.

Over the course of his seventy-six years, Eugene Walter was a writer, poet, editor, translator, cryptographer, puppeteer, and great cook (Clark 2001). Yet he has also been described as "the most famous man you never heard of" (Long 2002) and "one of the best kept secrets among fans of Southern food" (Hastings 2002). Walter was a multitalented individual who could turn any occasion into a memorable event. The parties he organized were legendary and endeared him to many people. Although he was perpetually impoverished, Walter was able to bring many different people together to create a type of social gumbo—a rich mélange held together by his creative imagination.

Walter was also well-known as a storyteller, his tales bordering on the unbelievable. One such story involved his receiving three pubic hairs as a Christmas present from actress Tallulah Bankhead, who was appearing in a Thornton Wilder play in New York City. Walter's talents even extended to musical composition. He once wrote and performed a love song about cholesterol ("cholesterol daahling I love you . . . without you daahling what would I do?"), which he dedicated to people who eat fatback (Upchurch 1989).

Walter possessed the ability to transform the simplest ingredients into a special meal, this despite the fact that he never had any formal culinary training. A case in point was a dinner he created in Paris for himself and a friend at a time when they were both destitute. The only ingredients they had between them were a few crackers, several onions, and a bottle of wine. He had only a small hot plate for cooking, plus several pans. With these limited ingredients and tools Walter was able to create a memorable meal that reflected the value of simplicity.

This resourceful and imaginative cook was born in Mobile, Alabama, on November 30, 1921. According to Walter (1991), he "was born and raised at the corner of Bayou and Conti Streets in the old downtown section of Mobile, that Gulf of Mexico port that was under Spanish, French, and British rule at various times, and the site of the first carnival celebration" (ix). For a number of years Walter and his parents lived across the street from his paternal grandparents (Walter

2000). Walter's mother, Muriel, suffered a nervous breakdown, however, when he was a young boy and was subsequently admitted to a psychiatric hospital. Following her discharge, she inexplicably moved to New Orleans. Aside from receiving a few cards without a return address, Walter never again heard from his mother (Walter 2000; Clark 2001).

Walter's father worked as a purchasing agent in the family business and had to travel extensively. As a result, Walter was raised primarily by his grandparents and lived in their Victorian cottage at 50 South Bayou Street. Like James Beard's family, Walter's grandparents set high standards for cooking as well as eating. Here is how he described life with his grandparents: "Everything in my early life was concerned with fine foods and wines, with gardening. I was in a kitchen and at a table forever" (Clark 2001, 15). Like M. F. K. Fisher, Walter was probably cooking up one thing or another most of the time. Walter characterized his grandparents as passionate gourmets who believed that in order to be a good cook one had to be a good gardener. He also noted that many "downtowners" had courtyard gardens and that few people purchased salad greens, tomatoes, and herbs from neighborhood shops (Walter 1991).

His grandparents' attitude toward food and cooking can be illustrated by the manner in which they cooked corn on the cob (Clark 2001). They grew corn in a small garden behind their house. Despite the fact that they employed a cook, his grandmother, who was called Ma-Ma, always took charge of this task. She would put a pot of water on the stove and then send his grandfather out to the corn patch. When the water was nearly boiling, she would instruct him to begin picking cobs off the stalks. As his grandfather shucked the corn, he would pass ears through the window to his grandmother, who would immediately drop them into the boiling water. The hot corn would be served with country butter. Fresh, locally produced foods thus became important to Walter, who later grew many of his own vegetables and herbs.

It was perhaps his grandmother who had the most significant impact on Walter's early life. He once described her as a "tiny woman with brown eyes, laugh lines, and clanking amethyst or amber or jet beads" (Walter 1971, 11). It was Ma-Ma who set the pace for each day. Her flapping slippers could be heard early each morning as she walked down the hall to the kitchen, where she fired up the wood stove and prepared the biscuits. Later in the morning the maid, Rebecca, would arrive and they would share the first cup of coffee. In addition to that day's gossip, their conversation would invariably include food. Each day seemed to be defined by the array of foods consumed at the Walters' table.

Both of Walter's grandparents had strong opinions about many different subjects and were never reluctant to express them. For example, Ma-Ma had advice for those who wished to avoid the sweltering summer heat. This was before the advent of air-conditioning. She insisted that one should go indoors and shut all the shutters and curtains, lie down on the sofa, and drink well-chilled champagne flavored with fresh peach while smelling a rose and having a foot massage (Upchurch 1989). It was from this interesting woman that Walter learned to love languages, and from whom he developed the desire to live abroad (Gee 1998).

Mobile, like the Portland of James Beard's youth, was a city in which food was an important element of everyday life. The daily routine was often punctuated by the sounds of food vendors. While pushing his cart down the street, the oysterman's voice rang out in the neighborhoods in which he sold his products: "Oy-ay-ees-oyster man, many-man, many-man, many-man!" (Walter 1971, 13). The iceman would arrive a while later, as would an assortment of different vegetable vendors, all contributing to the fabric of colors and sounds. These auditory, sensory, and visual stimuli combined to form what Walter described as scenes right out of *Porgy and Bess* (Clark 2001). Here was yet another example of gumbo in the life of Eugene Walter, a wonderfully flavorful mixture of people, sounds, and aromas. It was as though commerce centered around food, the consumption of which was an essential part of the city's pulse.

The rhythm of this interesting city permanently entered Walter's psyche. He described the sociable, front-porch atmosphere of his neighborhood, in which everybody knew one another so well that a simple gesture from a passerby might convey the message "I'm off to the market." The front porch thus became what Walter described as an extended family.

Many of the vendors passed the streets where their home was situated, creating, in Walter's words, a great levee (1971). Here his grandmother reigned supreme. She sat in her chair on their front porch, read the paper, shelled beans, and held court. She chatted with friends and neighbors and commanded the attention of nearly every person who passed their house.

Families of Mobile typically gathered at home for the midday meal, often napping afterward. The Walter family was no exception. The substantial meal invariably included rice and boiled greens, which were followed by a sweet course and fruit. On Fridays the family would also have fish at the noon meal. Walter's grandfather would often phone home to report that he found a particularly good piece of fish at the waterfront market.

Many people from the Mobile area revealed their affinity for food in their knowledge of when different types of products, such as butter peas, would be at their peak. For example, Rebecca might be the first to announce that the Crowder peas had come in, and it was often Walter's task to call out to passing vegetable vendors and purchase attractive-looking produce. Years later, when Walter shared a meal with Southern friends in one of the great restaurants of Paris, the after-dinner conversation invariably turned to what foods would be in season back home. The importance of eating regional foods also resonated with many other cooks, like James Beard, who emphasized the need to eat locally and in season.

The region in which Walter grew up was described by him as "south of the salt line" (Clark 2001, 6). This was an area he described as being a frontier between an "Anglo-Saxon South and a world which is a mélange of French, Spanish, English, and Confederate, with a thoroughbass of African and Indian" (6). He once described Mobile as possessing the culture of a French port and the home of the original Mardi Gras, a land of monkeys, clowns, ghosts, and musicians (Edge 2002).

After the stock market crash of 1929, the family business collapsed, and Walter's grandparents were forced to move from their familiar surroundings on Bayou Street to a rental property (Walter 2000). When Walter was only fourteen his father and grandparents had all died, leaving him orphaned. At that time he was sent to live with an older man, a Mr. Grayfer, who owned a chain of department stores. Several years later Grayfer died, leaving Walter both penniless and homeless.

With the strong current of old Mobile culture coursing through his veins, Walter left home at the age of seventeen (Edge 2002) He worked for a time as a tutor and artist in a forestry camp run by the Civilian Conservation Corps (CCC). Although the forestry camp was staffed primarily by boys from reform schools, Walter preferred this to being placed with a "Christian family."

After he completed his tour with the CCC, Walter moved back to Mobile, where he worked in a theater and a bookstore until he was drafted into the U.S. Army at the age of nineteen. In the army Walter received training as a cryptographer and was stationed in the Aleutian Islands located off the coast of Alaska above the Artic Circle. Despite the rugged existence, Walter continued to develop his cooking skills, which became a form of survival for a man accustomed to a cuisine more refined that that dished out in the army mess hall.

By early adulthood Walter had already developed a remarkable understanding of food. In fact, one of his letters about cooking at a New York restaurant was passed on to Lucius Beebe, a columnist for the *Herald Tribune,* who published it (Edge 2002). At the time of the letter's publication, Walter was only twenty years old. This was the same columnist who, a few years earlier, had written a positive review of a new catering business, Hors d'Oeuvres, Inc., that James Beard and his partners had launched.

After the war ended, Walter returned home and planned to move to New York City. He packed the essentials: a Remington typewriter, his stuffed monkey in a glass bell jar, and a box of gold paper stars he used to sprinkle on the stairways of his apartment building. The monkey and stars later became his trademarks. Over the years he collected a variety of gifts to his monkey donated by friends. When he wanted to compliment a female acquaintance, he often referred to her as the queen of the monkeys or a cat person (Edge 2002).

In New York City Walter initially worked in a rare-book store. He later moved to Greenwich Village and found work in the foreign-exchange section of the public library. He began to learn French and subsequently received a scholarship to study painting in a class sponsored by the Museum of Modern Art. He also worked in the theater as a set designer. As part of his duties, Walter began to construct puppets. During his brief stay in New York City, Walter earned a number of awards for his imaginative set designs.

For Walter, New York City was an incubator that permitted him to develop a multitude of talents. It was also the place where he formed a circle of lifelong friends, many of whom were artists and actors. The ability to establish and maintain a variety of friendships formed an important theme in his life. This group included the prostitutes who plied the street in front of his Paris hotel as well as the likes of William Faulkner and Judy Garland. He once referred to his close friends as an assemblage of cats and monkeys (Clark 2001). These connections served as a lifeline when he was down and out. At other times these friendships helped further Walter's career.

Many of these individuals became Walter's friends as a result of the inventive parties he threw. He possessed the unique ability to turn the most mundane activity into a festive event—on an extremely limited budget. An example of this talent is the time when, in Rome, he created an entire course out of broccoli in a casserole dish accompanied by Tabasco sauce served in a saucier.

New York City was indeed the place for a Southern boy to spread his wings and fly (Clark 2001). However, it proved merely a way station on Walter's journey to Europe. He had always wanted to go to Paris (Clark 2001). With little savings and future financial support from the GI Bill, Walter boarded a Dutch freighter and sailed for France to study art. And about the same time, a group of ex-GIs also traveled to Paris, later becoming classmates of Julia Child, who had recently arrived in Paris with her husband. Ten days later Walter was in Paris, feeling as though he were back home in Mobile (Clark 2001). He selected a small, inexpensive hotel in the Latin Quarter where Gertrude Stein, Molière, and Oscar Wilde had stayed before him.

Walter spent a total of three years in Paris, where his circle of friends continued to expand. He set up quarters in a small furnished room. Despite the fact that preparing meals on the premises was prohibited, Walter continued to cook for himself and friends. He later remarked that his landlords knew that he would keep his room clean—which he did (Clark 2001).

Paris was then a magical place for people interested in food. Joan Reardon (1994) is not exaggerating when she describes the culinary attraction of France as seductive. By the time Walter and the Childs had arrived, hordes of Americans had already discovered the cuisine of Paris. Waverly Root and A. J. Liebling, among others, had written extensively about their gastronomic excursions in that city. The latter, in particular, spoke of his time in Paris as an apprenticeship in eating (Liebling 1959), referring to a certain café as Root's "gastronomic secondary school" (115).

France thus became a laboratory in which Walter increased his knowledge about food and cooking. He explored every inch of France (Walter 1991). According to him, he "talked to ancient creatures in fields and woods gathering herbs and mushrooms, made an expedition into truffle country, interviewed famous chefs, sniffed out bakeries in back alleys, all that" (xi).

Many of these expatriates had only modest incomes. Nevertheless, they were able to take what Paris had to offer and create a virtual feast. Liebling captures the imagination in his descriptions of modest restaurants he discovered as he crossed "the modest threshold" (Liebling 1959, 112). Jonathan Bartlett, in his book *The Peasant Gourmet* (1975), captures the passionate sentiment attached to these Parisian experiences in his description of a simple French onion soup: "To the romantic imagination, this soup conjures up pictures of revelers in Paris ending up the wee hours in the hurlyburly of that great food market Les Halles, imbibing vast quantities of restorative soup" (16).

Crossing Walter's modest threshold, his guests entered a special world. His small room was decorated with stars on the ceiling and cutouts on the window to refract light across walls and ceiling. In this tiny room he served special dinners and parties for as many as twenty-five people. Each meal, made with only a few ingredients, became a special event.

Walter was not shy when it came to providing liquid sustenance to enliven the festivities. At a party he hosted in Rome for a visiting T. S. Eliot, for example, he concocted a version of his "23rd Field Artillery punch" that included two bottles of cognac, two bottles of white rum, and two bottles of very good English gin. He then filled the rest of the punch bowl with champagne. He later recalled that after a while, people "achieved a rosy view." At this particular party Walter "kept the glasses full" (Clark 2001, 190–91). After several glasses of punch, Eliot was chanting football cheers he had remembered from Midwestern colleges.

Creating special occasions thus became, in his words, a professional activity: "I work to give an interesting party. I like to make people meet people. I like to make people have dishes they have never tasted before. So, since I profess all of this, I guess I am a professional. I tried hard; I worked at it. After all, fun is worth any amount of preparation" (Clark 2001, 248).

While in Paris, Walter continued to write. He collaborated with a group of writers and editors, including George Plimpton, in the establishment of the *Paris Review*, where he served as an advisory editor for a number of years. By 1954 Walter had published his first novel, *The Untidy Pilgrim,* a humorous depiction of his hometown of Mobile, in which he contrasted his upbringing with the Puritan ethic popular in the United States (Hastings 2002). The novel subsequently won the Lippincott Fiction Prize (Clark 2001). During this period Walter also wrote a variety of articles on food for publications such as *Harper's Bazaar* (Hastings 2002).

In 1956 the GI Bill ran out and funds from the Lippincott Fiction Prize had been spent. Walter found his financial situation untenable. At the invitation of Princess Marguerite Caetani—founder and editor of *Botteghe Oscure,* which she published from 1948 to 1960—Walter packed his bags and left Paris for Rome, where he worked as Caetani's assistant. Walter's arrival in Rome marked the beginning of a long love affair with that city. In fact, he lived in Rome longer than any other place (Walter 1991). He moved into a small gardener's cottage, where he had a large rooftop terrace. The cottage was located high above the street, but the rent was affordable and the view of Rome through a trellis of grapevines was priceless.

As he had done in other locations, Walter created a special environment for himself. He planted fig trees along the path leading up to his home. On the terrace he grew herbs, okra, salad greens, tomatoes, and even pears. He also grew over fifty varieties of iris (Walter 1991). After spending six years in New York and Paris, Walter again discovered a place where cooks insisted on fresh ingredients. He felt at home in Rome because it was similar to Mobile in many respects.

One can only imagine what it must have been like for his guests to spend time with Walter on his rooftop terrace. He had access to an entire rooftop of produce, with the terrace floor blanketed with flowers (Clark 2001). Once beyond the threshold, one would discover a world in which good food, wine, and conviviality were paramount (Hastings 2002).

As he had done while in France, Walter scoured the country to uncover the subtleties of Italian cuisine (1991). The markets he visited throughout Italy must have seemed like a little bit of heaven on earth. The different foods—produce, fish, cured meats, cheeses, pastries—combined with the press of the crowd to create yet another levee—Italian style.

While in Rome Walter continued to write. In 1956 he received the Sewanee-Rockefeller Fellowship for *Monkey Poems* and in 1959 he was awarded an O. Henry Citation for *I Love You Batty Sisters.* His circle of friends continued to expand, including the likes of Italian film director Federico Fellini. On several occasions Walter attempted to interview Fellini for Rome's *Daily American* (Clark 2001), but Fellini was always too busy. After several appointments had fallen through, the director asked Walter to appear in a small role in his film 8½. He subsequently worked for Fellini as a translator and acted in several of his other films. For Fellini's film *Satyricon,* Walter spent nearly a year conducting research on foods as well as fabrics and dyes for the costumes. Throughout his career he appeared in scores of other films, including *The Pink Panther* and *Gidget Goes to Rome* (Edge 2002). He even appeared in an episode of *Saturday Night Live* as a restaurant patron who, after receiving an enormous check for his meal, dies with his face buried in a plate of spaghetti.

Throughout Walter's many years spent in Europe, he never abandoned his identity as a Southerner (Edge 2002). He once remarked that Southerners invariably return home not to die but to eat gumbo (Clark 2001). Walter even went so far as to take a small box of Alabama soil with him when he first ventured to Europe, stashing it under his bed so he would always feel he was sleeping on Alabama soil (Clark 2001).

In an introduction to Walter's book on Southern cooking, William K. Goolrick (1971), then an associate editor for Time-Life Books, described his first encounter with Walter in Rome. He noted the latter's enthusiasm for Southern food as having remained undiminished for over twenty years. Walter continued to entertain friends and acquaintances in an engagingly eccentric manner. His list of dinner guests included Judy Garland, Gore Vidal, and Truman Capote (Edge 2002). Someone once quipped that when visiting Rome there were two required activities: an audience with the pope and dinner with Walter.

It was with the perceptions of a "Southern Rip van Winkle" (Goolrick 1971) that Walter returned to the United States in 1971 to write *American Cooking: Southern Style* (1971), which was published by Time-Life Books. He found that much of the South he had grown to love had disappeared or was gradually slipping away. One such fixture of Southern life was the porch (Upchurch 1989). At a presentation he once gave, Walter described evenings spent on the porch. After supper, family members would quietly slip into their favorite chairs, armed with a beverage, while children would dart into the night to play hide-and-seek and other games. He recalled how a simple shoebox and candle could be transformed into a riverboat, with its lights shining in the evening, and the fact that there were often several of these miniature boats being hauled up and down the sidewalk on any given evening. The stillness of a quiet Southern evening may seem alien in our contemporary urban landscape. Is this now beyond our reach? Should our front porches be turned into cell phone–free zones?

The research for this book led to Walter's rediscovery of the South he had known as a youth and had revered throughout his life. It involved over five thousand miles of driving across the South and back again; since he did not drive, he was chauffeured in a station wagon.

From Maryland to the Florida Keys, Walter discovered and rediscovered the foods people cooked and ate in his cherished South. Not only did he collect recipes, but he also described the people who prepared these dishes, thereby preserving culinary traditions spanning generations.

For example, Walter explores variations in preparing fried chicken, which, in his words, "is as Southern as a mint julep" (1971, 42). He also discusses such issues as whether the milk gravy should be poured over the chicken or served on the side. He relates quirky, interesting stories about cooking chicken in the South that hold our attention, such as the Delmarva National Chicken Cooking Contest, where over seven tons of chicken were supposedly prepared in a frying pan measuring ten feet in diameter and eight inches deep.

In each section of the book Walter meanders through what has been traditionally called the "American South." At Monticello he serves up a brief, enticing biography of Thomas Jefferson, whom he characterizes as America's first notable gourmet. His narrative contains an overview of food-related gadgets invented by Jefferson, such as a rotating set of pantry shelves that permitted servants to pass food to diners from the kitchen through an opening without having to enter the dining room. In Jefferson's opinion, this minimized the possibility of overheard dinner conversations becoming servants' gossip. To augment his historical research, Walter arranged for a traditional "Jeffersonian dinner," which was organized by a representative of the National Trust for Historic Preservation. The dinner, normally held on April 13 (Jefferson's birthday), featured many of the foods and wines enjoyed by the third president and was served in Jefferson's own dining room.

When Walter decided to live in Mobile, the city lent him a home. It had been uninhabited for years and, in Walter's words, smelled like a "piss pie" (Clark 2001). He moved in with two cats that had accompanied him from Rome. Having repaired the damage caused by Hurricane Frederick, Eugene subsequently noted the destruction that thirty years of Baptists and bulldozers had inflicted on his native city. Old stately homes and historic buildings had been torn down, replaced by small, nondescript office buildings.

Upon his return, Walter had also received his beloved grandmother's cookbook from a cousin (Walter 2000). He continued to write, cook, and organize parties into his latter years. Walter also published several books, including *Hints & Pinches* (1991).

Having been immodest throughout most of his life, Walter followed suit and crossed life's threshold on March 28, 1998. It was said that his death was the result of both cirrhosis of the liver and cancer. The former was allegedly the result of a rather intimate relationship with "Dr. Jim Beam" (Hastings 2002). John T. Edge (2002) was right when he said that Walter had left us prematurely.

At Walter's funeral, he was eulogized by his cousin Francis X. Walter, an ordained Episcopalian minister, who stated that Walter had been blessed with a superabundance of joy and wonder (Walter 2000), adding that he had generously shared this gift with others throughout his life.

Francis Walter and his brother, David, saw to Walter's funeral arrangements (Walter 2000). David Walter transported the coffin to the local Masonic Lodge in his pickup truck. Paint and chalk were provided to mourners to decorate the coffin, which resembled a Mardi Gras float (Walter 2000). At his wake, friends and family gathered to share chicken salad sandwiches, port, and nuts—a meal of his choosing (Edge 2002). Walter's coffin was transported to the cemetery in the style of an old-time jazz procession. The man who was known as Mobile's Renaissance man (Sledge 2002) was buried in the historic Church Street graveyard. Although it had been officially closed since 1898, a mayoral "dispensation" made the interment possible (Sledge 2002). His headstone features carvings of a cat and a monkey.

Perhaps the most striking legacy of Eugene Walter was his ability to create special circumstances through the use of simple elements—including cooking. In *Hints & Pinches*, Walter best described his unique ability when he advised cooks to "seek fresh, avoid chemicals, keep a light hand, rise to the occasion, try what you don't know, have fun . . . and good eating you all!" (xiii).

References

Bartlett, J. 1975. *The Peasant Gourmet*. New York: Macmillan.

Clark, E. 2001. *Milking the Moon: A Southerner's Story of Life on This Planet*. New York: Three Rivers.

Edge, J. 2002. "Eugene Walter." In *Cornbread Nation 1*, by J. Egerton. Oxford, Miss.: Southern Foodways Alliance.

Goolrick, W. 1971. Introduction to *American Cooking: Southern Style*, by E. Walter. New York: Time Life.

Hastings, M. 2002. "Stories: Late Writer Knew Food, Enjoyed Life." *Winston-Salem Journal* May 1: 1.

Liebling, A. J. 1959. *Between Meals: An Appetite for Paris*. New York: Simon & Schuster.

Long, T. 2002. "Uncle Mame's Banquet." *Lambda Book Report* 10: 17–19.

Reardon, J. 1994. *M. F. K. Fisher, Julia Child and Alice Waters: Celebrating Pleasures of the Table*. New York: Random House.

Sledge, J. 2000. "The Enchanted Rooms of Eugene Walter." In *Moments with Eugene Walter*, by R. Barrett and C. Haines, eds. Semmes, Al.: KaliOka Press.

Upchurch, T. 1989. "Eugene Walter." Accessed August 19, 2004, at http://www.alabamastuff.com/walters.html. .

Walter, E. 1971. *American Cooking: Southern Style*. New York: Time Life.
———. 1991. *Hints & Pinches*. Athens, Ga.: Hill Street Press.

Walter, F. 2000. "MOMENTS/Walter." In *Moments with Eugene Walter*, by R. Barrett and C. Haines, eds. Semmes, Al.: KaliOka Press.

Susan Spicer

Resolute Dedication to a Craft

It's not just what Bayona brings to New Orleans,
but it is what Susan brings as a chef. She is not just one
of my favorite people in the world, but her love of food
has led her to a style all her own. She is active in the
community and is a real people person. She really
brings a glow to the culinary world here.
—Jamie Shannon, executive chef at
Commander's Palace, as quoted in
Amy Zuber's article "Bayona: New Orleans"

IN A CITY STEEPED IN TRADITION, including pride in its gastronomic heritage, Jamie Shannon's words are a tribute to the talent of chef Susan Spicer. When pressed to describe her work, Spicer modestly replies: "I am a working chef." Her response is not unexpected. Given the concentration and energy she brings to the kitchen, her accomplishments are also not surprising. She does not have time for labels such as celebrity or star chef.

Susan Spicer was born in Key West, Florida ("Persona" 1996), but was raised in the New Orleans region. Her father pursued a career in the U.S. Navy. As a result, Spicer's formative years were spent on a naval base as a "navy brat." She ate her mother's cooking and was "pretty much oblivious to local food and culture" (Zuber 1998). Spicer initially learned about cooking by watching others. It was from her mother that she developed an appreciation for the variety of foods available, since her mother was as likely "to serve fried chicken as curry" (Burros 1998).

After attending college for about a year, where she experimented with several different career paths including graphic arts, Spicer began working with a friend who was cooking professionally. She once remarked that her introduction to the industry occurred later in life—when she was in "her mid-twenties." Like many other accomplished culinarians, Spicer didn't have any formal, school-based training in the foodservice industry. Instead, she began as an apprenticeship to chef Daniel Bonnot at the Louis XVI restaurant in New Orleans (Zuber 1998). As Spicer later recalled, "I always felt as though I would probably end up doing something creative and food just happened to be the medium that I felt most comfortable with after trying a couple of different things. It just felt good. It felt natural." Bonnot became her mentor, challenging her to excel: "He was constantly pushing me to do things I hadn't done before." One of the duties of being a mentor, however, is to encourage a protégée to enter territory with which she is unfamiliar. Spicer credited Bonnot when she spoke of placing herself into situations that are not comfortable in order to grow and learn: "I realized that when I had done something at an event that was really, really challenging, and a lot of stress. Right while I was in the middle of the most stressful part, I am thinking: 'Why am I doing this to myself?' Then a little light bulb went off and said so that you will—so you will grow because you do not have Daniel to do this, to do these things anymore. It was a neat lesson to learn. It was a little point of clarity" (Spicer 2003). In 1982 Spicer completed a four-month internship at the Hôtel Sofitel in Paris, where she worked with chef Roland Durand (Spicer 2003). She returned to New Orleans and opened a sixty-seat restaurant, the Savoir Faire, located in the St. Charles Hotel (Zuber 1998), while continuing to work with Daniel Bonnot. After three years at the Savoir Faire, Susan traveled extensively through Europe and California; then returned to New Orleans in 1986 to open the Bistro at Maison De Ville (Spicer 2003). Spicer credits the knowledge she gained to both of her mentors (Simmons 2003). Her ultimate success, however, was also based on a love of cooking as well as a sense of determination, both qualities intimately bound up with her psyche.

In the eighties Spicer slowly emerged as the premier female chef in New Orleans. This was quite an accomplishment, especially given the fact that the residents of New Orleans are quite knowledgeable about good food. Thanks to her travels throughout Europe and California ("Bayona" 2004), her cooking reflects the varied flavors of the regional foods she experienced during her travels.

Spicer's style of cooking blossomed after she and her partner, Regina Keever, opened Bayona. The restaurant, located on rue Dauphine in the French Quarter, has become highly popular with a clientele that appreciates excellent foods. Its name reflects the Spanish name for the street, Camino de Bayona (Bayona 2004). As Spicer later recalled, "I liked the sound of the word. It was one of the first things I noticed about the building. I thought the name Bayona reflected the history, and it had a nice European sound to it" (Zuber 1998).

Setting herself apart from the Creole establishments of the French Quarter, Spicer offers an international cuisine Bayona's Web site, which captures this quality in the following quote by Spicer: "It's pretty much a melting pot, but it's not really fused." The restaurant's menu reflects this unique style, combining "hints of the Mediterranean, the Far East, North Africa, France, Italy and the whole of the United States" (Bayona 2004). It is represented in dishes such as grilled veal tenderloin with morels and English peas; creamy polenta and marsala-sage sauce; and pecan-crusted rabbit with stone-ground grits, smothered greens and Tabasco sauce. The composition of the menu, moreover, reflects a strong reliance on good-cooking fundamentals and the use of high-quality, fresh ingredients.

Michael Ruhlman

Charting the Course of the Craftsman

> I was in cooking school. Look at my houndstooth-check trousers,
> my big black heavy-soled shoes, my knife kit in hand, my leather
> briefcase over my shoulder—the symbolic combination of school
> and kitchen. I was going to learn how to make a perfect brown
> veal stock, the reasons it became perfect, and everything that
> followed from there.
> —Michael Ruhlman, *The Making of a Chef*

In Michael Ruhlman's book *The Making of a Chef* (1997) he includes a short memorial to the lasting memory he has of a granduncle named Bill Griffiths, who once wrote him a letter describing a meal he had ordered at Galatoires Restaurant in New Orleans. He recalled the wonderful cooked potatoes he had eaten. Not fancy, "the surfaces were delicately crisp and crunchy and the inside, rich, smooth and flavorful." Ruhlman concluded that the chef at Galatoire's "hadn't used the potato as a basis for displaying flashy, flamboyant skills, but had placed his skills as an artist in the service of the potato"(7). Like John Thorne, who wrote about savoring a simple dish of fried potatoes, Ruhlman attempts to uncover the learning involved in the creation of perfectly browned potatoes.

A successful writer, Ruhlman has published works on a number of topics—including the construction of wooden boats at Martha's Vineyard and the lifestyle associated with this profession. In addition to *The Making of a Chef*, he is the author of *The Soul of a Chef: The Journey toward Perfection* (2000). Together with Thomas Keller, a chef at the French Laundry, he coauthored the *French Laundry Cookbook* (1999). Most recently he collaborated with Thomas Keller and Susie Heller on *Bouchon* (Keller, Ruhlman, and Heller 2004), a book dedicated to the cooking served at bistros.

Throughout much of Ruhlman's work there is a persistent theme of honoring the work of craftspeople. In the manner of the chef at Galatoire's, perhaps Ruhlman inadvertently regards himself as an artist striving to master a craft. The contemporary craft of cooking in the United States reflects a number of conflicting attitudes.

On the one hand, chefs and "gourmet cooks" have considerable social status. In the home and in most commercial kitchens, the art of cooking has been diluted to a considerable extent. One only needs to walk through the corridors during the annual convention of the American Restaurant Association (ARA) in order to observe the momentous changes in the craft of cooking that have occurred in recent years. Technology and food-manufacturing processes have combined to reduce the skills needed by cooks in most restaurants. This is evidenced by the numerous food samples offered by these businesses. Fried appetizers, precooked chicken, and heat-and-serve soups can be found at booths throughout the convention. Many restaurants now base their menus primarily on the reheating of frozen foods.

While the craft of cooking does not need to be based on arcane knowledge, there is merit to the idea that excellence is frequently the result of an investment of time, talent, and energy. Developing an understanding of the fundamentals of cooking instead of having to rely on a combination of factory-produced convenience foods, gadgets, and cookbooks "for dummies" can also lead to excellence.

Ruhlman was born in Cleveland, Ohio, in 1963 (Ruhlman 2004). He attended Duke University and earned a bachelor's degree in English. After working for the *New York Times* as a copy boy for several years, Ruhlman traveled for a period of time, returning to Cleveland in 1991. In Cleveland he published his first book, *Boys Themselves,* about an all-male academy outside Cleveland (Ruhlman 2004).

Desiring to learn about the process of becoming a chef and developing a working knowledge of the fonds (basic procedures) of cooking, Ruhlman moved his family to Hyde Park, New York, in order to attend the Culinary Institute of America (CIA), a converted Jesuit monastery. Renting out the family home in Cleveland, they placed most of their belongings into storage and moved into "a one-bedroom garret above a garage in Tivoli, New York" (Ruhlman 1997). For nearly two years they commuted twenty miles to and from the institute.

The process of completing a traditional culinary education such as that offered by the CIA is complex—especially for someone with a family. In addition to the traditional classroom-based education, students work in skills laboratories (blocks at the CIA) for up to twenty hours per week. This process is intellectually, emotionally, and physically challenging. Ruhlman explained that the school rarely shut down: "The first class, A.M. Pantry, or breakfast cookery, begins at three-fifteen in the morning, about four hours after the last class of the previous day ends. There are twenty-one blocks in all, eighty-one weeks including externship" (Ruhlman 1997).

The narrative of Ruhlman's book *The Making of a Chef* (1997) is therefore based on an intense, lived experience. He had originally planned to participate in the school environment as an observer but was soon caught up in the battleground of a commercial kitchen (Ruhlman 2004). Just as Rick and Deann Bayless decided to explore Mexican cuisine and culture, so Ruhlman invested a substantial amount of time, energy, and resources into understanding the craft of becoming a chef.

The Making of a Chef describes Ruhlman's experiences as he struggles with both a novel curriculum and a different way of cooking. Having a sense of how to prepare food in a home kitchen is of little or no use when it comes to working in a commercial kitchen. The hospitality industry poses special challenges, such as long hours. At one point in the book, Ruhlman interviews chef Michael Pardus, his skills instructor, who complains about never having time off on holidays.

Ruhlman gained insight into the difficult and challenging routine of a chef when he informed Pardus that he could not attend classes because of the terrible weather conditions. Pardus insisted that Ruhlman be there irrespective of the weather: "Part of what we're training students to be here is chefs—and when chefs have to be somewhere, they get there" (Ruhlman 1997, 68). Ruhlman packed his equipment, and although he arrived late, he successfully completed that day's assignment.

I experienced a similar situation while taking the culinary skills block at Grand Rapids Community College. I was commuting approximately forty-five miles and had to be in the classroom adjacent to the kitchen at 7:00 A.M. sharp. It was January, pitch-black, with heavy snow falling, when my car suddenly skidded off the two-lane highway. Fortunately several other drivers stopped and helped me get back on the road. When I arrived late, Chef Muth gave me a puzzled look and asked why I was on the road on such a day. When I replied that I needed to be in the kitchen for my skills test, he shook his head and said no examination was worth that kind of risk.

While Chef Muth appeared more tolerant that Ruhlman's instructor, the fact remains that hospitality personnel have to be on the line even during extremely difficult conditions. For one thing, the "products" purchased by most hotels and restaurants cannot be inventoried and sold the next day. If a seat in a restaurant remains empty at 7:00 P.M. on any given night, the opportunity to make a sale is lost forever.

As part of the initial educational routine at the CIA, Ruhlman was asked to perform repetitious tasks: "Everyone would cut two pounds of *mirepoix*, one part each of celery and carrot, two parts onion. And we would do this every day for the next six weeks" (Ruhlman 1997). This repetitive work develops basic skills, such as the ability to handle a chef's knife (without earning the nickname "stubby"), and gradually leads to what Noah Adams (1997) has characterized as the shift from novice to expert. Ruhlman later described the rigorous process of competing for master chef certification (2000), noting how one candidate's ability to perform complex tasks automatically helped her make up time lost earlier in the day: "Lynn begins by boning four Dover sole. She can do this in her sleep, and the sheer mechanics of it lead her mind back to the kitchen" (31). Poaching a Dover sole for use in a terrine may not form part of a home cook's repertoire. However, consider the value of preparing food with a few simple techniques—stewing, baking, grilling—without having to constantly refer to a cookbook. Repetition thus adds to the cook's skill and increases her sense of mastery.

Another set of formative culinary experiences for Ruhlman in this initial block involved learning through tasting. Chef Pardus instructed his students to learn to cook with their senses—eyes, nose, and ears. A case in point occurred when he had Ruhlman ladle out some vegetable soup and add salt in order to taste how this altered the flavor.

Chef Angus Campbell has used the same instructional technique. For example, he would tell students to listen for the "rattle" of the chutney as it simmered as a way of knowing if it is finished. Likewise, Rick Bayless has recommended the use of sensory information—the aroma of cooking oil or a shimmering appearance on the surface—to determine if oil is hot enough for frying. While these methods appear to be quite useful, there are still many cooks who are tied to recipes with predetermined cooking times, who, for example, need to use a timer to know when their pasta is al dente.

A number of other lessons were packed into this block, but one theme consistently recurs in the first part of Ruhlman's book, namely, the need to invest time, energy, and talent to achieve mastery of a craft. This is evident from a short chapter in which Ruhlman sketches the career path of his instructor, Chef Pardus. The latter had entered the CIA in his early twenties and had worked in a number of positions while refining his skills and adding to his knowledge base. Like many other people in the field—Julia Child and James Beard come to mind—Pardus experienced a meal that constituted a defining point in his career. It is important to mention that he also experienced his sciatic nerve being "blown out" while cleaning thousands of shrimp for a buffet at a hotel in New Orleans where he worked.

Despite the hard work, Ruhlman also experienced a considerable degree of satisfaction related to his progress. Although the mentally and physically demanding work can easily wear a person out, there is always the sense of satisfaction of finishing and remaining on one's feet. Few people who have not worked as a cook "on the line" can appreciate this feeling. There are times when the line of tickets seems to fade over the horizon and you're in a territory called "the weeds." It's then that you draw on all your emotional, intellectual, and physical resources and begin to dig yourself out of the hole one plate at a time. At the end of the shift, your feet ache and you are coated with sweat, not to mention a number of other substances. Still, there is always that moment when you realize that you faced a considerable challenge and survived.

This sense of satisfaction would be meaningless if it were not measured against a set of standards to which craftspeople such as Pardus use as a way of assessing the quality of their work. These standards were applied to the learning process of Ruhlman and his fellow students. Everything had a standard of quality against which something was to be measured. For example, consommé was judged on the basis of aroma, flavor, body, and clarity—the latter defined as the ability to read the date on a dime at the bottom of a gallon of the soup.

This, then, is a way of viewing the journey of the craftsperson. It is no coincidence that the word "journeyman" is also based on the same root word. Michael Ruhlman uses his own life, as well as the lives of accomplished craftspersons, to illustrate the endless path toward culinary mastery.

Given her personal commitment of time, energy, and considerable talent, it is not surprising that Spicer and Bayona have received national, if not international, attention. Recognized by the James Beard Foundation as best chef in the Southeast in 1993, she was voted chef of the year in New Orleans in 1992. Bayona received a Four Diamond award from the AAA in 1995 and was named one of the best restaurants in the world by *Restaurant Magazine.*

In order to fully appreciate Spicer's contributions, however, it is important to look beyond the awards and the publicity. As her reputation has risen in the culinary culture of New Orleans, she has become a role model and mentor for a number of women who aspire to the profession of chef. She also gives classes in her restaurants and reaches out to the general public.

When Spicer speaks of teaching and learning culinary skills, she acknowledges the need to understand basic principles. "I can tell you, okay, when you sauté something, here's the things you need to know: hot pan, dry food, don't crowd the food and bring the temperature down, blah, blah, blah, it's got to sizzle and all that stuff" (Spicer 2003). However, as with Rick Bayless, Spicer points to more fundamental changes as a result of learning to cook. There has to be an assimilation of information in order for the cook to act automatically.

To move from having to think about each and every step of the cooking process to doing it reflexively is a sign of growing expertise. This path is often challenging and can sometimes be quite brutal. The arena of the kitchen is not a place for calm feedback and thoughtful discussion. It is a dangerous workplace filled with sharp objects, fire, boiling water, and hot oil. Spicer is emphatic about her kitchen staff being able to accept criticism without becoming defensive, which she feels is an essential component of the learning process in the kitchen.

Another important element of Spicer's teaching is that she cares about the people with whom she works. As a result, there is a feeling of nurturing that is most likely the result of her own experiences as a novice. As she recalled, "I cried a lot at Savoir Faire, but I learned how to handle the responsibility—and timing—of running a restaurant." People in the kitchen are always expected to perform at a certain level. This ideal is reflected in the words of chef Angus Campbell, who theorizes that a person in a high-quality kitchen might be instructed to poach a twenty-pound salmon for the next day's service. If the salmon were not poached to perfection, that person might be gone the next day. Spicer wants her staff to remain open to new possibilities as a way of continuing their growth in the craft of cooking: "Over the years, as I learned more, I started to assimilate a lot of information. Some stays with you, and some you discard naturally. And then one day, lo and behold, you have a style" (Zuber 1998).

Spicer's impact on the local community is another important aspect of her professional life. She has provided seminars on cooking to community groups and helped to open a specialty shop, Spice Inc., that sold carefully selected ingredients and cooking utensils. In the spirit of its motto ("Food is our passion"), the shop featured lunch service, an online store, special-event catering, and cooking classes. Guest chefs such as Rick Bayless offered cooking demonstrations as well as classes to provide participants with hands-on experience (Bayona 2004).

Although the shop closed after only two years of operation, that single business reflects only a small part of Susan Spicer's connection to the New Orleans community. She regularly shops the local

Crescent City Market and makes sure her menu is based on ingredients that are fresh and easily available. Spicer has also served on the board of the market (Kamerick 2002). Like Chicago-based celebrity chef Rick Bayless, she also seeks out artisan producers of special foods, thereby raising social capital by promoting special knowledge about various foods.

All this has been accomplished by a quiet, determined woman in a city that is known for its flamboyance (Burros 1998). When people hear New Orleans, they immediately think of its raucous French Quarter district. Visited annually by revelers who come to experience the excesses of Mardi Gras, the French Quarter has earned its reputation as a place where nearly anything goes. This permissive spirit is certainly promoted by a variety of tourist-oriented businesses nestled in the French Quarter that pander to the exotic tastes of visitors from out of town.

There is, however, another aspect of the French Quarter that often remains invisible to the casual visitor. If you get up early in the morning and walk the streets of this district, you can watch as it recovers from the previous night's revels. There is a wonderful stillness where recently there was noise and even chaos. Delivery trucks pull up in front of eateries, while workers pick up the debris of the previous night's celebration. It is too early for the hustlers and panhandlers. Fortunately, the last of the celebrants vanish as the streets are washed clean, and life begins anew in the French Quarter.

This tourist attraction is also a neighborhood. The people who live within the confines of the French Quarter, an area covering approximately forty to fifty square blocks, share a sense of community. The shopkeepers, bartenders, clerks, and cooks tend to recognize the regulars who inhabit the area. With its concentration of writers, artists, and musicians, the "neighborhood" may sometimes resemble Toole's *Confederacy of Dunces* (2000). However, there is still a tangible sense of belonging here. Many of the long-term residents know Spicer personally and address her by her first name. Thus, both her name and the name of her restaurant, Bayona, have become part of the French Quarter culture.

References

Adams, N. 1997. *Piano Lessons: Music, Love & True Adventures.* New York: Delta.

"Bayona Restaurant." 2004. Bayona. Accessed January 2, 2005, at http://www.bayona.com.

Burros, M. 1998. "The Quiet Star of New Orleans." *New York Times.* Accessed April 8, at http://www.housemedia.com/spiceinc/nytimes/htm.

Kamerick, M. 2002. Women of the Year 2002: Susan Spicer. *New Orleans City Business* 23: B47.

Keller, T., and S. Heller 1999. *The French Laundry Cookbook.* New York: Workman.

Keller, T., M. Ruhlman, and S. Heller. 2004. *Bouchon.* New York: Artisan.

"Persona: Susan Spicer." 1996. *New Orleans Magazine* 30: 13.

Ruhlmann, M. 1997. *The Making of a Chef.* New York: Henry Holt.

———. 2000. *The Soul of a Chef: The Journey Toward Perfection.* New York: Viking.

———. 2003. Personal interview with author. July 28.

———. 2005. "Michael Ruhlman." Accessed January 5, 2005, at http://www.ruhlman.com.

Simmons, S. 2003. A Woman's Touch. *New Orleans Magazine* 37: 81.

Spicer, S. 2003. Personal interview with author. July 23.

Zuber, A. 1998. Bayona: New Orleans. *Nation's Restaurant News* 32: 112.

Carlo Petrini

Creating Space for Individuality in a World of Mass Production

> We are enslaved by speed and have all succumbed to the
> same insidious virus: Fast Life, which disrupts our habits,
> pervades the privacy of our homes and forces us to eat
> Fast Food. . . . Our defense should begin at the table with
> Slow Food. Let us discover the flavors and savor of regional
> cooking and banish the degrading effects of Fast Food.
> —Adapted from the Slow Food Manifesto
> in Peter Jones et al., "Return to Traditional Values?
> A Case Study of Slow Food"

IF FARMERS' MARKETS and their customers protest against a
factory system of food production and its accompanying assembly-
line lifestyle, they will find solace in the work of Carlo Petrini, the
president and cofounder of Slow Food. Petrini was born on June 22,
1949, in Bra, a small town in the Piedmont region of Italy. From an
early age he was surrounded by the foods, wines, and traditions of the
region and exemplifies the intimate relationship many Italians have
with their local produce. This spirit pervades Petrini's organization
as well as the Slow Food movement as a whole (Kummer 2002).

These foods and wines of Piedmont are not what one might
describe as "gourmet." The Slow Food movement has developed
an emphasis on foods that are part of people's daily lives, not those

associated with Michelin-rated restaurants (National Public Radio 2004a). In fact, Petrini (2001) has stated that the wines "in his blood" (2) were made in the courtyards of urban apartment buildings, not in the great houses of Barolo. Quoting the writer Velso Mucci, Petrini remembers strong aromas from vats of must from small hillside vineyards punctuating the fall season, like the smell of burning peat that marks the passage of winter in rural Scottish communities of the Western Isles. It was this rural community, with its small-scale farming and a tanning industry, that in Petrini's words struggled into the seventies. Yet in this community there also arose a tradition of organized social groups: "Catholic, laic or socialist" (3). It was from the heritage of these cooperatives that a loosely knit organization called Arcigola evolved in Bra with the goal of promoting wine and tourism in the area (Petrini 2001). It had originally been part of a larger organization, the Associazione Ricreativa Culturale Italiana (ARCI), a left-leaning national recreational association. Petrini was put in charge of the gastronomic wing of the organization (Stille 2001).

Early in the eighties Petrini and his associates founded a small restaurant, the Osteria del Boccondivino, located in the old section of Bra (Petrini 2001; Kummer 2002). This restaurant, which is still in operation, is situated on the second floor and faces a modest courtyard. Walking up the wooden steps, you feel as though you are entering your grandmother's kitchen. It is warm and inviting. The hardwood floors and tables add to the comfort, with the windows looking down onto the courtyard. Across one long wall, there is a large collection of wines. The food and wine menus are uncomplicated and affordable. The service is quiet and professional. This is certainly an atmosphere that draws your attention away from the outside world. The Osteria del Boccondivino is a place where you want to spend a lot of time.

It was here that Petrini and a number of friends discussed food, wine, and the preservation of their local culture. In 1986 Arcigola developed out of these conversations, and its establishment was celebrated with a dinner in the courtyard that ended only with the break of dawn (Petrini 2001). Organizers of Arcigola also published a little guide to wine, Gambero Rosso (Red Shrimp), whose name hints at the organization's political stance. At first little more than an insert "dedicated to food and wine" in the "left-wing daily *Il Manifesto*" (Petrini 2001, 7), the publication was later expanded into a highly successful guide to the wines of Italy called *Vini d'Italia* (Gambero Rosso 2004; Petrini 2001). The eighteenth edition of the guide was presented to the public in a ceremony during the 2004 Salone del Gusto, a biannual international celebration of food sponsored by Slow Food. By 1990 the latter had expanded its publishing program and launched the Slow Food Editore (Petrini 2001).

In the old section of Bra, where the Osteria del Boccondivino is located, you cannot help but experience the character of small Italian communities. In doing so, you can appreciate the essence of the Slow Food organization and the movement it has engendered. Located in the same neighborhood is the Caffe Conversa, another quiet establishment that is part of Slow Food culture. It consists of a few tables and a small patio. A good place to socialize over a glass of wine, it was here that Petrini and a few friends met in 1986 to decry the construction of a McDonald's outlet at the foot of the Spanish Steps in the Piazza di Spagna in Rome (Jones et al. 2003). This piazza, named for the Spanish embassy for the Holy See where it is located, is a cultural icon in Rome. The protest that ensued resulted in what has come to be known as the Slow Food Manifesto, which argues that "a firm defense of quiet material pleasure is the only way to oppose the universal folly of Fast Life" (Stille 2001). Following a conference held in Paris in 1989, Slow Food became an international movement. Just as quiet conversation in inns and other public places throughout the American colonies helped spark a revolution, the meetings at the Caffe Conversa jump-started a movement that has rapidly spread across the globe.

Situated several blocks from the café, up a narrow street, is the headquarters of the Slow Food organization. Slow Food offices occupy an assortment of buildings in the center of Bra. Unlike the nondescript buildings in landscaped corporate parks where many American businesses are located, the headquarters of Slow Food is situated in a comfortable space that feels homey. Although it is difficult to describe exactly what this movement represents, it is impacting our lives daily. While it was initially developed as a form of rebellion against fast food (Jones et al. 2003), there is much more to the movement. Richard Owen (2000), for example, portrays Slow Food as a much broader phenomenon "whose leitmotifs are anti-globalisation, anti-standardisation and the assertion of local and regional identity" (Owen 2000).

Perhaps Slow Food's most critical role is to encourage people to become more aware of the foods they routinely eat. In addition, it wants the public to examine the social dimension attached to food consumption. What occurs between people at the table? Do the sounds associated with digesting one's food replace conversation? This is an important issue in the United States, where a staggering number of individuals gulp down chow at fast-food outlets or eat while driving or watching television. This frenetic pace leads people to consider food as simply a form of fuel for their biological engines. The adage "eat to live, don't live to eat" reflects not only a mechanized approach to food but also a puritanical attitude toward what should be one of the greatest sources of pleasure in life and a fundamental right of all people.

Evidence of this mechanized attitude can readily be found in the fast-food outlets that dot our highways and serve as "fueling stations" for busy commuters. The practice of locating scaled-down versions of fast-food franchises alongside gas stations and inside convenience stores is widespread. In addition to purchasing fuel for her car, the harried consumer can also purchase heros (subs), tacos, hamburgers, and fried chicken for her body—much of which is gulped down as she commutes in her automobile. For an even quicker fix, there are always doughnuts, candy bars, potato chips, and cookies. Perhaps the most alarming aspect of this phenomenon is that consumption of these foods appears to be routine.

The Salone del Gusto and Terre Madre

Celebrations of Artisans, Wine, Food, and Cultural Identity

> Imagine a village with lots of colored streets, where each corner
> is vibrant with people, colors, voices and aromas. Imagine being
> able to meet hundreds of food artisans who describe history,
> tradition and culture through their products.
> —(Salone del Gusto 2004)

Each spring the U.S. National Restaurant Association (NRA) holds its annual convention at Chicago's McCormick Place. For over eighty-five years restaurateurs have traveled across the country and around the world to attend an event that is spread over two million square feet of exhibition space.

Tens of thousands of people flock to this major event, crowding downtown restaurants and filling up hotels. Over two thousand vendors pay over twenty-five dollars per square foot of space, vying with competitors both large and small for the attention of hordes of people who march past their booths each day. Considering the rental costs, the amount of floor space needed by many of the large vendors is amazing. For example, one vendor incorporated an entire semitrailer rig into his display.

One way food vendors have attracted the attention of attendees is by offering complimentary samples. The massive quantity of free food available represents a drawing card for the show. The free foods offered reflect consumer interest in various segments of the restaurant industry, known as quick service, quick comfort, and casual theme. The foods offered by operations within these segments, moreover, point toward a heavy reliance on foods that can be prepared quickly by semiskilled employees. The result is a mind-boggling array of factory-produced frozen and partially prepared foods that can be baked, microwaved, or deep-fried to order.

When one factors in the cost of renting floor space, food samples, and salaries, participation in the show can be quite expensive. It is therefore hardly surprising that the major venues are operated by large, multinational corporations. These organizations obviously possess the capital needed to participate in such an event. They also have the products and technology demanded by an industry built on speed and simplicity—one that has been highly successful in transforming traditional concepts associated with restaurants into feeding factories.

In Europe another major food event has been taking place for approximately nine years, one that is also attracting the attention of food lovers across the globe. In the Lingoto Exhibition Center in Turin, Slow Food and Italy's Piedmont region have created a forum in which small producers from around the world have come together to celebrate artisanal foods produced primarily on a small scale. Aptly named the Salone del Gusto (Hall of Taste), this is a venue where, for example, you can encounter a Scottish family selling their blue-veined cheeses, a small-scale operation that produces cold-pressed olive oil in Liguria, or a Spanish producer of cured meats who ages his hams for up to three years. Not simply a marketplace where consumers can purchase exotic foods, the Salone del Gusto provides a forum where vendors communicate a sense of history, tradition, and culture through their products (National Public Radio 2004a). Like the market on Floyd Boulevard, only on a grander scale, this is where producers and consumers find a common ground to celebrate the best life has to offer.

The first Salone del Gusto took place in 1996 (Petrini 2001). According to Carlo Petrini, unlike traditional wine and food fairs, this initial event stressed regions, products, and artisans. This was, in Petrini's words, a small experiment aimed at educating the public taste primarily through taste workshops.

The initial event featured foods from many different local producers. Above all, it provided a platform for the Slow Food movement to promote locally produced foods, regional culture, and artisanal knowledge. It proved so successful that Slow Food made a commitment to conduct it every two years (Petrini 2001). Petrini was able to convince managers at Fiat to permit the event to take place at their Lignotto building. Enzo Ghigo, president of the region of Piedmont, provided strong support for the initial project. In 2004 he characterized the Salone as one of the region's most important promotional initiatives, which, since 1996, "has managed to generate a small cultural transformation by shifting the focus of attention from industrial machines to the gifts of nature" (Ghigo 2004). Turin, with its long tradition of automobile manufacturing, is considered by many the Detroit of Italy. Thus, the Salone represents a significant shift within the culture of Piedmont from an industrialized society to one that is more culture-bound and regionally specific.

Over the course of three subsequent Salones, the event has assumed epic proportions. The 1998 Salone was substantially larger than its predecessor, featuring over three hundred producers of regional foods (Petrini 2001). The Salone also had an impact on Italian agricultural policy, helping to improve the status of small-scale agricultural producers.

In 2000 the Salone continued to expand. There was now an emphasis on biodiversity. Slow Food established a foundation for biodiversity that intended to preserve the artisanal heritage worldwide (Petrini 2001). By 2002 over 2,000 registered journalists participated in the event, and over 140,000 people attended taste workshops (Petrini 2001).

The 2004 Salone witnessed expanded participation. In all, nearly 150,000 people attended. The Buon Paese Marketplace, which has been described as the heart of the exposition (Salone del Gusto 2004), occupied over 105,000 square feet of exhibition space and included over 400 vendors from all corners of the world.

This marketplace also included over 190 protected Presidia products. The inclusion of the latter embodied Slow Food's emphasis on protecting biodiversity and regional identities. Cacaos from Ecuador were offered by indigenous peoples dressed in traditional attire. The presence of artisans, small-scale farmers, shepherds, and harvesters, all combined to create a unique atmosphere reflecting the strength of regional cultural identities.

This marketplace was a lively arena comprised of long aisles through which crowds of people from around the world strolled. Three aisles were filled with cheese vendors. Other aisles included meats, seafood, fruits and vegetables, spirits, spices, oils, and vinegars (Salone del Gusto 2004).

In addition to the Buon Paese marketplace, Slow Food sponsored an enoteca (wine cellar) where participants tasted wines and paired them with a variety of foods—fish, vegetables, and cheeses. Over twenty-five hundred labels were offered. Taste workshops represented yet another venue in which taste education was promoted. Participants paid nominal fees to take part in a wide variety of taste experiences. For example, on one specific day in October taste workshops included: 1997, Year of Barolo; The World of Rice; and Genoa's Great Confectionary Tradition. In all, thirty-two workshops were held that day.

To augment the taste workshops, Slow Food sponsored a series of events called the "Theater of Taste." This component of the Salone featured such celebrities as Alice Waters, whose presentation focused on organic foods. Other presenters included an expert on the Andean cuisine of Argentina and a demonstration of New Basque by a chef whose family has managed an award-winning restaurant since 1897.

Other opportunities for tasting were provided in an area dedicated to the foods of a number of Italian regions, such as the Veneto and Campagnia. The latter, for example, set up a small restaurant and offered three minicourses paired with wines from the region—all at no cost to attendees. This and other components of the Salone demonstrate the close-knit relationship between Italians and their regional foods. In an interview with Sylvia Poggioli of National Public Radio (2004b), one attendee described his experience of tasting Barolo, a wine from his native region. He stated that the wine's flavor, color, and aroma all reminded him of home, adding that one needed to grow up near the vineyards in order to appreciate how the grapes are transformed through the seasons. Regrettably, this knowledge is often lost in a fast-food nation such as the United States.

Since Slow Food is an international movement, an entire area was dedicated to world kitchens. This area featured cooking demonstrations that emphasized traditional techniques and regional products. Food from around the globe, including northern Africa and Latin America, were available for tasting at a "World Tables" area. Slow Food has described the opportunities for taste experiences in this area as follows:

> At the World Bistro you will be able to taste Indian Basmati rice or compare badda beans from Polizzi with black beans from Toulouse, beef from Welsh Black and Podolica cattle, maize dishes from various parts of the world (from polenta to tamales and tortillas), ice cream made with Mananara vanilla, with Cacao Nacional from Ec-

uador, with chestnuts dried in tecci or with lemon from Amalfi. To finish off, a cup of coffee—choosing between Huehetenango (Guatemala), Dominican Republic and Chiapas (Mexico)—or a cocktail of guaranà from Saterè Mawé. (Salone del Gusto 2004)

Other events featured at the 2004 Salone included the Master of Food Program. This multiyear initiative in taste education is "dedicated to gastronomic culture, with presentations of the history, traditions, production processes and distinctive features of various foodstuffs" (Salone del Gusto 2004). One program in particular was designed to teach young people about the historical and cultural aspects of food as well as its sensory component. One workshop, where children learned about the nature of rice kernels (National Public Radio 2004a), was designed to instill a sense of culinary knowledge and an appreciation for good food. Children also had an opportunity to examine the lives of small-scale farmers (Salone del Gusto 2004). Armed with this knowledge, it is hoped that children will be better equipped to resist the lure of greasy fast food.

In short, the Salone del Gusto has made Slow Food a global phenomenon (Kummer 2002). The international impact of this event was illustrated in a number of taste workshops, where simultaneous translations were provided in several different languages.

The 2004 Salone was accompanied by a parallel event that also reflected Slow Food's emphasis on understanding the link between gastronomy and food production. The Terre Madre: World Meeting of Food Communities was held around the corner from the Salone in the Palazzo del Lavoro. It was attended by over five thousand producers of foods from around the world. According to Slow Food, the event created "a forum for those who seek to grow, raise, catch, create, distribute and promote food in ways that respect the environment, defend human dignity and protect the health of consumers (Terre Madre 2004).

Terre Madre was specifically established to permit communities of producers, artisans, distributors, and retailers to collaborate in preserving small-scale, typical food production (Petrini 2004). This vibrant event included food producers from over 130 countries who represented over 1,200 different food communities (Petrini 2004).

According to Sylvia Poggioli of National Public Radio (2004), the venue was filled with unique producers, such as Tibetan yak herders, Native American wild-rice harvesters, Masai foragers, and Chilean blue-hen farmers.

Through workshops and discussions, these groups from different continents, speaking many different languages, discovered ways in which they could reduce their isolation in a world that has become increasingly industrialized. They also shared strategies to deal with a common enemy: multinational agribusiness. Prince Charles of Britain, who addressed the conference, spoke of the regrettable trend of imposing industrial farming on traditionally agricultural societies. This practice has the potential to destroy both biological and social capital while eliminating cultural identity, whose roots lie in working with the land.

At the end of the event Carlo Petrini (National Public Radio 2004b) addressed the participants. He passionately asserted that when they returned to their villages—whether in mountains, plains, or valleys—they would no longer feel isolated. He proposed that the network created at Terre Madre would provide farmers with a sense of strength and would lend dignity to their work. Bill Coleman, an organic farmer from Santa Barbara, California, reported that as a result of the event, he felt proud to be a farmer, to be part of a bigger consortium of human beings engaged in small-scale, sustainable agriculture. He emphasized the positive aspects of farms as places suitable for raising families.

Sergio Chiamparino, the mayor of Turin, spoke of (2004) Terre Madre as presenting an opportunity to reflect on our future in terms of the quality of the food we eat and how it is produced. This necessitates a heightened awareness of the conservation of biodiversity, the thoughtful use of natural resources, and the assurance of dignified working conditions for all people. These ideals are shared by Gianni Alemanno (2004), the Italian minister of agriculture, who underscored the need to place small-scale producers front and center rather than large multinational corporations. It is for these reasons that the city of Turin, as well as the region of Piedmont, committed substantial resources to facilitate the creation of Terre Madre. It is now up to consumers worldwide to confront the challenges posed by this unique event.

Food consumption may not fit neatly into a busy schedule. After all, active people may not have the time to share a leisurely meal with family members. Slow Food encourages people to begin to consider those activities they choose to pursue and how they affect the quality of their lives. Of paramount importance, according to this movement's philosophy, is savoring the moment and living in the present. We need to remain in control of how we choose to spend our time and resources. These important decisions should not be made by corporate executives of the fast-food and retail industries.

According to Slow Food advocates, a thoughtful and sensitive approach to life is based on our capacity to slow down. And slowing down should not be limited to food and its consumption. It can and must become a way of life. Drawing from the works of the Italian writer Francesco Angelita (Slow Food 2004), Slow Food's spirit is captured by the snail, which is their logo. Angelita wrote about snails in the sixteenth century. Remarking that man has much to learn from this creature, he stressed that "being fast makes man inconsiderate and foolish." This stands in stark contrast to the frenetic lifestyle promoted in modern industrialized cultures (Owen 2000). By moving more slowly through life, Slow Food advocates believe that we create more opportunities for nourishment of both the body and the mind.

Adopting a slower lifestyle also provides us with opportunities to improve the quality of our nutrition. When people sit down together at the table and eat slowly, they have sufficient time to experience the feeling of satiety and are less likely to overeat. Likewise, when we prepare our own meals, we become conscious of the ingredients that are consumed. We can exercise such options as deciding what foods to include in our daily diet, determining portion sizes, controlling how our food is to be prepared, and avoiding excessive quantities of things like sugar and salt. When we dine out—especially at fast-food outlets—many of these decisions are made for us.

Another important element is the sense of accomplishment we

feel when we can prepare a meal "from scratch." Cooking becomes a craft that instills a sense of pride in us. The process of cooking can also generate social networks in which people prepare food together while discussing this important aspect of their lives.

Cooking for ourselves thus becomes an integral part of our identities. As we develop into more proficient cooks, we are able to teach others about the craft. When we do so, our knowledge increases and we create social capital. This knowledge contributes to a just society. The alternative is to remain drones in a mechanized society.

Mass marketers want us to believe that modern, successful people do not have the time to prepare and enjoy meals, that we and our children are far too busy. Such a belief is not readily accepted by dieticians, who point to the fact that the average American watches twenty-two hours of television per week (Entering 2003). Father Dominic Garramone adds that while many people contend that they have no time to bake, they often do so during holiday periods, when there is even less time.

Another important Slow Food theme concerns an appreciation of where foods originate. This is not simply a matter of tracing where food has been produced but a fundamental concern for the regional identity of foods and cultures. Coupled with this concern is a strong belief in the use of sustainable products. Members of Slow Food work to preserve local products and traditions. A case in point involves the effort by the U.S. branch of Slow Food to revitalize the harvesting of Delaware Bay oysters, once an important cash crop for residents of the southwestern New Jersey shore (Chadwick 2002). This effort was accomplished by addressing such major issues as environmental impact, while also putting harvesters in touch with consumers. In addition to preserving products such as the Delaware Bay oyster, Slow Food strives to protect recipes as well as harvesting and production methods (Chadwick 2002).

One way in which the Slow Food movement has been able to preserve local food traditions is by exercising its political leverage. When the European Union attempted to enforce public-health requirements that favored large-scale manufacturers, Slow Food was able to create enough pressure to enable the Italian government to offer exceptions for small-scale producers of artisanal foods.

By stressing the importance of regional foods and traditions, Petrini and the Slow Food movement are combating what they perceive as a process of homogenization promoted by manufacturers of mass-produced foods. Members of Slow Food have argued that the consumer does not benefit if a piece of provolone tastes the same in Chicago, Budapest, or Beijing. They have also warned that when multinational corporations sell their standardized commodities worldwide, they also steamroll culture (Petrini 2001).

An emphasis on locally produced foods and regional characteristics also carries with it a concern for the environment as a result of overproduction, the reduction of cruelty to animals, and the promotion of humane work environments. Slow Food promotes local, free-range methods over what have been described as "factory-farming concentration camps" (Chadwick 2002). This focus also involves being aware of how people who produce these foods are treated on the job. The ultimate goal of Slow Food is to make consumers more aware that the beef they are purchasing may be produced in a factory where workers are routinely overworked or otherwise abused. They then have the option of not purchasing these products.

A cornerstone of the Slow Food movement is the convivium, or local chapter. According to their materials (Slow Food 2004a), the term is based on the Latin words meaning "with life." However, it also has other, more subtle connotations. The word also refers to the Roman term for dinner party. Similar words in English include "convive," an eating companion, and "convivial," meaning to be fond of feasting. Each contains the all-important element where people are drawn together through the act of sharing food.

There are over eight hundred convivia worldwide, with approximately half located in Italy (Slow Food 2004). Slow Food clearly states that these convivia are "the linchpin" of the movement. These local, grassroots organizations represent the philosophy of Slow Food to their local communities (Slow Food 2004). Each convivium has its own character (Chadwick 2002). For example, members in Australia have been purchasing old homes in the Barossa region and restoring their characteristic wood-fired bread ovens (Harri 2004). In Scotland a Slow Food member has collaborated with a local chef to organize visits to a vegetarian restaurant by local schoolchildren, who help prepare a meal (Pearson 2003).

The leader of a local convivium, known as the fiduciary, works with Slow Food's national office to coordinate events such as workshops that highlight local food specialties and traditions. These events enhance public awareness of local foods and traditions, especially those that may be endangered. This could, for example, involve an invitation by a local cheese producer, who would demonstrate how cheeses are produced using raw milk, followed by a tasting session. Such a session would promote both knowledge of artisanal methods of food production and sense knowledge.

Activities organized by a local convivium should also promote "moments of conviviality" (Slow Food 2004). During such activities people are encouraged to step off the Fast Food treadmill in order to savor life. It is this social aspect of the convivium that seems to be most compelling. When people break bread together and socialize over food in a convivial manner, they help defeat the popular habit of eating quickly and—frequently—alone.

This same phenomenon occurs when people prepare food together, as in community kitchens. For example, Wendy Priesnitz (2003) points to the community kitchen as a place where people share skills, socialize, and reduce food costs through collective purchasing. In the eighties Patti Zwick and a number of friends in Quincy, Illinois, formalized this concept by creating a food-buying club. Originally conceived for a few families who pooled their resources in order to buy food in bulk and save money, the small group quickly expanded to include several hundred people. The monthly delivery of food became a social event, and communal meals quickly ensued.

In conjunction with this widespread convivium network, Slow Food has produced a number of ingenious and ambitious initiatives. In 1996, at the inaugural Salone del Gusto, Petrini and a group of colleagues formed what they referred to as the Ark of Taste (Petrini 2001). According to Petrini (2001), this consists of "scholars of gastronomy, sociologists, political scientists and gourmets" who met to discuss the loss of competent craftspeople and the disappearance of a large number of fruit and vegetable species. Petrini summarized the fundamental outcome of this discussion as follows: "Faced with this situation, Slow Food set out a concrete proposal with a symbolic name, the Ark, because the ark is what we need to save quality food production from the flood of standardization and its blighting effects" (85–86). Petrini called this "the Noah Principle."

If one visualizes Noah escorting pairs of animals into a large wooden vessel to protect them from the rising waters of a global flood, we can catch the spirit of the Ark of Taste. The rising waters are of a different ilk but are just as threatening. They include industrial standardization, laws of hygiene, the regulations of large-scale distribution, and environmental damage (Petrini 2001).

At first the number of products contained in the Ark of Taste was modest. However, by 1999 it included nearly five hundred different products, and the number has swelled as the initiative has spread to a variety of countries, including the United States (Kummer 2002), where products include the Crane melon, the Delaware chicken, and the elephant heart plum (Kummer 2002). The Ark of Taste thus represents a concerted worldwide effort on the part of Slow Food members to preserve food products as well as traditions and knowledge that are on the brink of extinction.

The spirit of the Ark of Taste reveals an interesting facet of Slow Food, namely, its ability to make use of powerful imagery and to engage the public. In order to further the goals of the Ark of Taste, for example, Slow Food created the Presidia initiative (Petrini 2001; Kummer 2002). The term is based on "presidium," which means fort or garrison, another powerful symbol that evokes a strong emotional response. Through the activities of the Presidia, Slow Food marshals its resources to protect threatened forms of food and artisanal knowledge. In the case of the Delaware Bay oyster, Presidia representatives act as "mini SWAT teams" to link producers of these special products with cooks and the general public (Kummer 2002).

Another initiative that has drawn on the capacity of Slow Food to capture the attention and imagination of the public has been the Osterie. This program, which has its roots in traditional Italian eating establishments, first emerged in the form of a guidebook, published by the Slow Food Editore, entitled *Osterie d'Italia*. The osterie program reflects the importance of regional identity. The restaurants marked with the snail logo provide simple, traditional food at moderate prices that reflect local produce. This program is in direct opposition to the current practice of awarding stars to fancy restaurants, as well as the strip-mall mentality of chain restaurants that situate "eateries" offering the same food in any neighborhood worldwide that will support them.

Among the numerous small restaurants in this guide, Di Maria is typical. If you walk through the winding alleyways of the Carugi district of Genoa, you may find yourself facing this small restaurant nestled in a very narrow alley off a busy street. There are taller buildings on either side, so this is not a place for claustrophobics. Inside, different-size tables placed fairly close together occupy two floors. The noise level during the midday meal is pronounced but the atmosphere remains convivial.

The crowd that frequents Di Maria is heterogeneous and includes young couples, large groups of businessmen, and laborers. The food and the conversation combine to create an inviting atmosphere. This is not your usual sterile foodservice establishment with a menu based on a thoroughly researched marketing plan. Instead, the service is quiet and friendly, and the food consists of good, solid, homemade fare.

An example of the food offered at Di Maria is pasta with a simple pesto. The pesto carries the strong flavors of its ingredients—olive oil, fresh basil—and was invented in the region. The pasta and other selections are served using plain dishes, and the house wine is provided in small pitchers. For a modest sum a person can, as the Acadians in the United States are wont to say, pass a good time with friends at Di Maria.

A few miles from Genoa, another osteria located in the town of Seralunga d'Alba is La Rosa Dei Vini. It sits atop a hill and looks out over a valley whose contours are carpeted with grapevines. The menu is different from that available at Di Maria. For one thing, it is printed as opposed to the daily handwritten bill of fare at Di Maria—and it is somewhat more expensive. The wine list here is much more extensive, reflecting the location of the restaurant in the heart of a wine region that produces the likes of Barolo, Barbaresco, and barbera.

The service at La Rosa Dei Vini is also different. Perhaps it is somewhat more formal, given that its rural setting does not result in large numbers of customers. When I last visited, I escorted a group of seventeen university students enrolled in a study abroad program. We sat at a single table while the husband-and-wife owners served lunch. It was a pleasure to watch how they choreographed the service as they delivered food, removed empty plates, and deftly poured wine from decanters. Here again the sense of efficacy and pride in being able to master the skill and knowledge needed to serve such a large party was on display.

What both Di Maria and La Rosa Dei Vini demonstrate is what Petrini and others have called *terroir* (Petrini 2001). This combination of natural and social factors produces a unique character and a sense of locality. Despite the dramatic differences in location, both Di Maria and La Rosa Dei Vini provide the opportunity for people to direct their attention away from the hustle and bustle of modern life in order to focus on more important matters.

In keeping with its stress on education, Slow Food has established the first university of gastronomic sciences, with campuses in Polenzo and Colorno. The university's first students arrived on campus in the fall of 2004. The first class consisted of over seventy students from around the world (National Public Radio 2004a). A three-year undergraduate degree is offered in addition to a two-year master's degree.

A cornerstone of the university's programs is an extensive array of *stages*, or internships. Many of these are international. The *stages* provide practical application of theory-based learning and deal with various categories of food products, such as cheese, coffee, and cured meats. *Stages* take place in different regions of Italy as well as other areas around the globe, including India, Ireland, Sub-Saharan Africa, and Mexico.

The small size of the student population at the university fosters close contact between students and faculty. Students from all over the world are encouraged to apply, with the basic admission requirements including mastery of English and Italian. Both Italian campuses are situated in rural areas and are close to food-growing and wine-producing regions.

Educational efforts of Slow Food are also furthered through a number of publications overseen by Slow Food Editore. These include the periodicals *Slow Magazine* and *SloWine*. An important aspect of Slow Food Editore is their guides, which include such titles as *Italian Cheese, Osterie 2004*, and *L'Italia del Pane* (traditional Italian bread). Slow Food Editore has also entered the travel market. These guides, *Ininerari Slow*, include destinations such as Cinque Terre and the Gulf of the Poets. Finally, Slow Food Editore's guides to wine include their longstanding *Vini d'Italia* as well as such interesting references as the *Wine Atlas of the Langhe*.

These publications, together with a variety of initiatives, complement each other by enhancing the fundamental goals of the Slow Food movement. The themes of this movement—regional identity, environmental sustainability, human dignity, and the right to pursue pleasure—interweave to create a complex tapestry. This movement has the potential to confront some of the most pressing challenges of modern life.

References

Alemanno, G. 2004. "A Necessary Experiment." Bra, Italy, Slow Food. Accessed November 27, at http://www.terramadre2004.org/welcome_en.lasso.

Chadwick, B. 2002. "Easy Does it." *E Magazine* 13: 42.

Chiamparino, S. 2004. "Thinking to the Future." Bra, Italy, Slow Food. Accessed November 27, at http://www.terramadre2004.org/welcome_en.lasso.

"Entering a 'Slow Food' State of Mind." 2003. *Tufts University Health & Nutrition Newsletter* 20: 1–2.

Gambero Rosso. "About Us." 2004. Accessed September 4, at http://www.gamberorosso.it/portaleEng/noi/.

Ghigo, E. 2004. "Salone Del Gusto." 2004. Accessed November 26, at http://www.salonedelgusto.com.

Harri, S. 2004. "Back to Basics: Slow Food—It's Also Good for Your Soul." *The Advertiser* [Adelaide, Australia] February 21: 29.

Jones, P., et al. 2003. "Return to Traditional Values? A Case Study of Slow Food." *British Food Journal* 105 (4–5): 297–305.

Kummer, C. 2002. *The Pleasures of Slow Food: Celebrating Authentic Traditions, Flavors and Recipes.* San Francisco, Calif.: Chronicle Books.

National Public Radio. 2004a. "Saving Slow Food in Turin." Accessed November 25, at http://www.npr.org/templates/story/story.php?storyId=4157137.

National Public Radio. 2004b. "Slow Going: Rolling Back the Tide of Processed Food." Accessed November 25, at http://www.npr.org/templates/story/story.php?storyId=4185366.

Owen, R. 2000. "A Slow Death for Fast Food?" *The Times* [London] October 27.

Pearson, L. 2003. "Chew on This Slowly." *The Scotsman* [Edinburgh] 6/12: 16.

Petrini, C. 2001. *Slow Food: The Case for Taste.* New York: Columbia University Press.

———. 2004. "Four Days in Step with the World." Bra, Italy, Slow Food. Accessed November 27, at http://www.terramadre2004.org/welcome_en.lasso.

Priesnitz, W. 2003. "Communal Food." *Natural Life* 5/1: n.p.

"Salone del Gusto." 2004. Bra, Italy, Slow Food. Accessed on September 4, at http://www.salonedelgusto.com/eng/pagine/01_mercato_paese.lasso?-session=carrello:9CC1FFE6120F82FFFAAD4178692F67E9.

"Slow Food: All About Slow Food." 2004. Bra, Italy, Slow Food. Accessed on August 30, at http://www.slowfood.com/eng/sf_cose/sf_cose.lasso.

Stille, A. 2001. Slow Food. *The Nation* August 26: 11–16.

"Terre Madre: A World Meeting of Food Communities." 2004. Turin, Italy, Regione Piedmonte. Accessed on November 27, at http://www.terramadre2004.org.

Angus Campbell

A Hundred Thousand Welcomes from a Passionate Teacher

> If you show passion and love for the food you are creating, people will understand what it is worth. . . . I have spent my whole life working with food to get to the point of showing you how to make bruschetta with bread, garlic and olive oil, and I love what I am doing and I am excited about showing you this. That has to tell you something.
> —Chef Angus Campbell, interview with author September 8, 2003

ONE SUMMER I PLANNED to introduce the art of making sausages to students in several hospitality- and tourism-management classes I offer at our university. I called several butcher-supply companies for advice on such things as equipment and supplies and even visited one of them. I knew that I was in the right place when the sales clerk informed me that "Chef Angus shops here."

Chef Angus Campbell is a culinary instructor at Grand Rapids Community College in Michigan. He offers a production class in which students learn how to prepare lunch for the Heritage Restaurant, which is operated by the Hospitality Education department at the college. His contribution, however, goes above and beyond the management of a kitchen. Campbell provides leadership as well as inspiration, serving as both a role model and mentor for his students.

When patrons lunch at the Heritage Restaurant, the food they eat is far from ordinary. The menu changes constantly, offering varied fare to regular guests from the college as well as the larger community. Typical choices might include grilled jerked red snapper, shrimp and mango curry, and lamb tagine with artichoke. Chef Campbell creates this interesting menu together with a group of twelve to fifteen relatively inexperienced culinary students, who spend a total of eight weeks in his kitchen, after which he begins again with a new group.

Campbell conducts his classes with determination and passion. There never appears to be a trace of boredom in his voice as he explains various details in his kitchen. His task, as he sees it, is to instruct culinary students in two major areas: the fonds de cuisine, which consists of the basic skills of food preparation, and the discipline necessary to function as a professional chef. According to Campbell, these are "key building blocks for success, especially in a subject that involves complex skills" (Cooking 2004). The latter, he adds, become automatic as students master the craft. Campbell insists that his mastery of these skills provided the basis for his rank as a chef. He bases his overall proficiency on both his mastery of these skills and the degree to which his students learn them. That is to say, he sees their mastery of the basic skills he teaches as an indication of his own competence as a craftsman—both as chef and educator.

Campbell was born and raised on Lewis, one of the Western Isles (formerly called the Outer Hebrides) off the coast of Scotland, whose Gaelic name, Leodhas, means marshy (Internet Guide 2002–3). Over a hundred miles in length, the island's varied topography includes picturesque beaches as well as fresh- and saltwater lochs (Internet Guide 2002–3). Lewis is also home to Scotland's equivalent of Stonehenge.

The Hebrides have long been considered a center for Gaelic language and culture. Gaelic is an important part of Campbell's identity. His television show uses the Gaelic expression "Céad Mile Fáilte," (a hundred thousand welcomes) as part of its logo. The greeting reflects Scottish hospitality, a spirit that is consistently demonstrated in Campbell's manner of collaborating with students and colleagues and in the way he treats customers.

The island of Lewis is connected to another island named Harris. Lewis has a population of over six thousand, most of whom are concentrated in and around the main port of Stornoway (Isle of Lewis 2004). It was there that Campbell attended Laxdale Junior Primary and Secondary School, as well as the Nicholson Institute, the equivalent of an American high school.

It was on this picturesque yet rugged island that Campbell's parents settled in the fifties. It was there, in the region famous for Harris Tweed, that they managed a small weaving business out of their home. Although one usually thinks of Paris, New York, and Rome as the traditional "breeding grounds" of chefs, Lewis produced a remarkable chef, passionate teacher, and proud Scotsman.

Life on the island was, in Campbell's words, very basic. He spent much of his childhood in a close-knit rural community. His father built their home at about the same time he was born. It lacked central heating and was heated by peat moss. Food was prepared using a stove that relied on the same source of energy. Campbell's mother made regional specialties like bannocks, a type of Scottish bread leavened with baking powder. When the dough was cut into farls (wedges), the finished product resembled scones. She also made oatcakes, which were thin, crisp toasted rounds of oat.

Absent from the Campbell kitchen were devices such as microwaves and convection ovens, bread machines, and other gadgets now common in contemporary kitchens. The Campbells also fared quite well without such convenience foods as frozen pizza, precooked pasta, and gravy mixes. According to Campbell, the food was hearty. His passion for his mother and her cooking is reflected in his remark that no one could equal her scones and fresh croudie (a simple white cheese), which were produced without any state-of-the-art appliances. Campbell had many opportunities to help with cooking, and this must have sparked his interest in the craft.

The use of peat moss in the Campbell home reflects the character of family members' lives. Imagine rising on early winter mornings and huddling around the peat-fired stove until the fresh peat logs reheated the room. Family activities were organized around such basic aspects of life, which Americans tend to take for granted. Shopping for food at the nearby supermarket or convenience store or ordering pizza in were simply not options.

The Campbells possessed the necessary resources to be self-sufficient. For example, they had access to fresh butter and maintained a beehive for honey. They also tended their own garden. The family was part of a close-knit and supportive community. When it was time for the Campbells to mine their peat moss for the year, other families would help, with the Campbells willingly reciprocating. Cutting and drying peat was an annual ritual within these communities. Cutting blocks of peat from the bog is tedious and demanding work—and that is just one of several stages in this process. These collaborative efforts became social gatherings, meals were cooked communally and shared. This resembles America's rural heritage, when families would band together to harvest and shuck corn or perform other labor-intensive tasks. Activities such as these drew people closer together and strengthened communities.

The lifestyle of the Campbell family was not one of impoverishment, but it was nevertheless very practical. A case in point is the butchering of sheep, where the entire animal was used. Campbell was fascinated by the various activities associated with this process, such as watching an old man deboning their lambs. One is again reminded of African Americans, who traditionally used all parts of a pig.

Foods produced in the Campbell home were labor-intensive. The family hardly depended on any premade food. Based on traditional recipes and a unique cultural heritage, these foods were typically prepared using locally produced ingredients. The Campbells ate a variety of soft and hard cheeses. Salmon, cod, and herring were also plentiful, as were an assortment of vegetables and fruits. They prepared puddings and meat pies, stews, layered casseroles (called stovies), soups and broths, as well as an assortment of breads and preserves. Naturally, they also ate shepherd's pie and haggis.

Each day the Campbells would leave a bucket at the gate, and the delivery person from a local dairy would fill it with milk from a churn. The Campbells knew that if the milk were left out too long, it would sour. However, they had a number of recipes that called for soured milk and thus nothing was ever wasted. Every morning a van would deliver fresh bread from Stornoway. When they opened the van door, steam would pour forth and they would peel off loaves of the warm bread. For the Campbells, products such as milk, cheese, and bread were not items produced in distant factories. They knew the people who made their food.

Much of the food preparation was accomplished at the Campbell's kitchen table, with the children watching. This created a lasting impression that honored the practice of cooking for the entire family. To this day, Campbell takes pride in the food he prepares for his family, and neighborhood children know that the pizza he helps them bake in his outdoor, wood-fired oven is a special treat.

Campbell has described how his mother made blood pudding at the kitchen table and how he was fascinated by the entire process. Like the Appalachian families described by Sidney Saylor Farr (1983), the kitchen table served as the center of family life.

Campbell thus grew up with people who were very close to their food. He recalls that he was always helping with the cooking and handling food. He wasn't repulsed at having to fillet a herring because he had done it hundreds of times each summer. This provided him with a sense of confidence that he readily imparts to his students. It is evident when he talks about preparing red snapper, which is based on the fact that he has fished, caught, cleaned, "and cooked it on 20 beaches in the Bahamas" (Campbell 2003).

Cooking was an integral part of the daily routine in the Campbell household. According to Campbell, "It had to be done, three times a day" (Campbell 2003). The end result was good, nutritious food.

An example is clutey dumplings, made from a batter consisting of fruit, nuts, flour, and baking powder. Campbell's mother would butter the inside of a pillow case and coat it with flour. The batter would be poured in and the case would be loosely tied. It would next be placed into a pan of water, topped with an upside-down plate, and covered with a lid. The mixture was then poached, drained, and cooled.

Baking with a peat-fired stove required the cook to be attuned to heat level and other factors without the benefit of a thermostat or other device. This process was similar to baking practices in mid-nineteenth-century America, where recipes would include directions such as "bake in a quick oven." Campbell learned to gauge the oven's heat by observing how long the fire had been active and how much peat was on the flame. This knowledge had been transmitted to him by his parents, who had learned it from their parents. Campbell has characterized it as having "touch, feel and experience." Today he passes along this same knowledge to students and even to children in his neighborhood, who learn to bake their individual pizzas on a stone hearth without the benefit of a thermostat. He has taught them that the best tools they can apply to the art of cooking are their individual senses combined with an active imagination.

This knowledge is vastly different from the way in which people living in the United States typically learn to cook, although such family traditions nurtured generations of cooks until the twentieth century. Now cooking schools, cookbooks, gourmets, and celebrity chefs have become the repository for cooking knowledge. Currently much of our cooking is either handled by machines, such as microwaves, or is performed by restaurant chefs. Although we enjoy the meals, they seem divorced from the simple pleasures associated with preparation of the food itself. We have all regretted the fact that our grandmother never revealed the secret recipe of her cinnamon rolls or how to make hot chicken-noodle soup from scratch on a cold winter's day.

The Greater Grand Rapids Food Systems Council

Enriching Community Food Networks

It's not just about the apple. It's about the person behind
the apple. It's about the farm worker who picked
the apple. And the farmer.
—Tom Cary, "The Greater Grand Rapids Food Systems Council"

Just as Angus Campbell teaches his students about the importance
of fresh, locally produced food, so Tom Cary and a dedicated group
of activists based in Grand Rapids, Michigan, have also invested their
time, talent, and energy in promoting small-scale, local food producers through a just and sustainable food system for their region.

In 2002 thirty-five food-security activists, farmers, and alternative food systems advocates met to establish an organization that
would educate residents of three counties in western Michigan
about locally produced foods (Cary 2005). Three areas of concern
were identified: education, access to local foods, and marketing for
local producers.

Over the course of its first year of operation, the council inau-
gurated a five-part educational series called Food for Thought. The
series covered such topics as gleaning, community gardening, urban agriculture, and food practices (Cary 2005). The council also
established a small farmers' market that served over two thousand
customers in its first year, channeling over eight thousand dollars in
profits to local, small-scale food producers.

With a membership consisting of chefs, environmental and religious organizations, planners, farmers, community gardeners, con-
servationists, educators, and health professionals, the council has
achieved a number of goals. Council members have joined together
to organize community gardens in the Greater Grand Rapids area
and are drafting an urban agriculture policy paper. Members are
also working with the Kent County Emergency Needs Task Force
Food Subcommittee to provide support to the pantry system soup
kitchens and the Second Harvest Gleaners (Cary 2005). The council
has continued to support the local farmers' market and has initiated
plans to create a downtown market "that will serve as a hub for

food-systems education, food-business entrepreneurship, food-arts training, food brokering and distribution, and year-round access to local food boutiques and restaurants" (Cary 2005).

Future plans include the establishment of a connection to the Slow Food network. At present, an application for a local convivium has been drafted. Members of the new convivium have made plans to support independent, locally owned food producers, markets, and food-service operations. They are also planning to promote local foods and are organizing a number of food-related events for members. Like the Slow Food Editore, the council plans to publish a *Western Michigan Local Food Guide* that will be available online.

The Greater Grand Rapids Food Systems Council is representative of a loose network of similar organizations across the United States and Canada. These organizations reflect a broad-based concern for the industrialization of the food system. However, like Slow Food they are not simply reactionary in nature. They seek to make consumers aware of alternative options regarding food acquisition. This necessarily involves challenging habits created by decades of mass-marketing efforts on the part of large-scale food producers. In doing so, these organizations will enrich our lives and strengthen our communities.

When Campbell turned sixteen and was old enough to work outside the home, he seized upon the opportunity to work part time at a local hotel as a porter. The father of one of his friend's had built the hotel and had helped him to obtain the position. After a period of several months, the hotel manager asked Campbell if he were interested in working in the dining room, and he eventually ended up in the kitchen. He found this work so interesting that he subsequently left school in order to pursue a career in the culinary arts. After working in various kitchens on the island for several months, he set out for the Scottish mainland.

It was here that Cambell began his formal training in the culinary arts. Initially he worked at the Rothes Glen Hotel in Moray Shire, which is located near a number of whiskey distilleries and fishing villages along the coast. Part of an old baronial manor, the hotel offers fine dining. (Campbell has profited from his early experiences at the Rothes Glen Hotel and features a fish entrée called Walleye Rothes Glen in his television series on cooking.)

Work at the hotel was challenging. During his stay of nearly three years, Campbell managed each section, or station, of the kitchen. These included: *garde manger* (cold-food preparation), fish, saucier, roast, soup, vegetable, and pastry/bake shop.

Campbell next moved down the coast, where he worked at The Tufted Duck Hotel, situated on the historic Buchan coastline of Aberdeenshire. Traditional Scottish cuisine is served in its three dining areas. He later recalled that this was one of the most challenging moves of his life, given that the cultural differences between the northeast coast of Scotland and his home in the Western Islands were so great. It was here that he began to learn the craft of teaching while supervising and training kitchen staff. He also oversaw recipe development, menu design, and food production.

Campbell's experiences parallel Slow Food's emphasis on regionality. How many people outside Scotland are aware of the fact that regional cultural differences in this small country could generate so much anxiety in a youth? Slow Food insists that if we leave the matter of regionality to chance, individual characteristics will vanish, leaving us with images of golf players, bagpipes, haggis, and the caber as representative of Scottish culture.

During this period Campbell continued to travel within Scotland, working in the cities of Elgin, Aberdeen, and Ayrshire. Wherever he found himself, he continued to remain open to the experiences around him—and he expects no less of his students. It was, as he recalled, a stage of his life punctuated by an unstructured series of positions, with each offering him opportunities to learn. This is similar to the informal type of apprenticeship many chefs undergo in the United States. Michael Ruhlman and Anthony Bourdain have both described the process whereby aspiring chefs work for accomplished craftspeople, accepting minimal wages in the knowledge that the ultimate payoff is experience. In each position these aspiring culinary professionals develop greater expertise, building upon what they initially learned in culinary school.

Despite the fact that Campbell moved around a lot, he continued to engage in repetitious tasks that contributed to his becoming a knowledgeable professional. For example, he might have made stock, sauces, and desserts on a daily basis. By working in this manner, the basic skills of cooking became second nature to him. This type of work was also demanding, and performance standards in the kitchen were high. The young cooks worked the breakfast shift through midafternoon, returning to work through the dinner shift and late into the night. There was also the expectation that the young chefs perform at a high level. According to Campbell, one might be presented with a twenty-pound salmon to poach for the next day's buffet. The expectation was that the salmon would be prepared to perfection and ready for serving. If this was not the case, the person involved might be dismissed the next day.

By 1976 Campbell was engaged in more formal training unavailable through employment. Through the guild system in basic cookery, he learned about cooking for the catering industry, advanced dining-room techniques, and advanced kitchen skills and *garde manger*. In this "working college" he attended classes for three months at a time. In the intervening periods, he and his fellow classmates would have "block release time," during which they worked in commercial kitchens. Once he completed a course such as *garde manger*, he would receive a diploma. He received credit for his studies through Moray College of Education and Glasgow College of Food Technology.

Working under this guild system, Campbell acquired the skills necessary to perform as a professional chef. His training reflected centuries-old traditions associated with food production. Nowadays tradition is all too frequently abandoned as many academic institutions pursue cutting-edge techniques and compete to be "more wired." However, without the sense of identity that only tradition can bestow, everyone may eventually receive "McDegrees." Campbell eventually achieved the master craftsman level of certification in his field in the Craft Guild of Chefs. He was subsequently awarded a professional teaching diploma from Jordan Hill College of Education in Glasgow.

Campbell was only twenty-four when he began teaching culinary arts at Glasgow College of Food Technology. In this capacity he promoted the fundamental skills he had learned through his apprenticeship and his restaurant work, while also developing his skills as a counselor.

After working at the college for over eight years, Campbell left Glasgow to assume the leadership of the Bahamas Hotel Training College in Nassau. Here he supervised the staff of the college and ran a national apprenticeship program. From the Western Islands to the Scottish mainland and on to the Bahamas, Campbell had traversed a considerable amount of cultural territory in a relatively short period of time. In the Bahamas he discovered local residents who, like his family, relied on produce grown in their own small gardens. Today, when Campbell teaches his students about such foods as bird peppers and jerked chicken, he speaks with the authority derived from having taken the time to learn about the local people and their traditions while simultaneously developing an understanding of their foods.

Campbell left the Bahamas after three years, arriving at Grand Rapids Community College in January 1991. His initial responsibilities included teaching a banquet and catering class, where he was able to inspire students to create sophisticated banquets for a variety of events. He would stress the need to develop a special atmosphere for the participants. It was up to the imagination, talent, and energy of the class to create this special atmosphere.

The annual madrigal banquet that students in Campbell's classes organized is a case in point. The event included faculty and students from the college's theater department. Every aspect of the banquet was well planned. Foods reflected the cuisine of the Middle Ages, and each table was assigned its own "knave" to serve the "lairds" and ladies. Costumes reflected fashion of the period, and the room was specially decorated for the occasion. The highlight of the banquet had Campbell leading a torchlight procession of servers bearing a whole roasted pig on a great platter.

At Grand Rapids Community College Campbell has conducted international tours for students and has encouraged students to apply for international culinary internships. He has also taught seminars on international cuisine and has served as a coach on a number of culinary teams in different competitive events.

In addition to his teaching responsibilities, Campbell has taped a series of programs that have been produced and broadcast by the community college. For example, in one episode he demonstrates how to bake walleye fillets in a backyard brick oven, while in another he and a colleague from the Bahamas demonstrate how to prepare authentic Bahamian dishes.

Campbell's teaching style reflects the strong influence of tradition imparted to him by his family and gained through his work in a number of different cultures. An example of this is reflected in his comments to culinary students about preparing savoyarde potatoes (pommes de terre à la savoyard), where he takes the time to explain the context in which these potatoes were prepared and consumed. He talks about the importance of Parmigiano Reggiano to the culture of northern Italy and the role of this potato dish in the celebration of this cheese. In doing so, Campbell reflects his belief in regional differences and the unique cultural heritage promoted by Slow Food. By incorporating this element into his teaching, he avoids simply teaching recipes to students and he is able to convey the spirit he feels for his subject.

One major influence on Campbell's narrative style of teaching derives from his early exposure to Elizabeth David. When he was still an apprentice, he had to write a paper on Mediterranean cooking and picked up David's book on the subject. He later recalled that he admired her ability to bring the region alive, the fact that she talked about people and places in addition to discussing the food of the region. Now Campbell also brings food and cooking to life for his students.

Campbell also stresses the importance of simplicity in cooking. He challenges learners to create interesting dishes with just a few simple ingredients and insists that foods should be allowed to cook "naturally." When I was enrolled in his class, this was called "the gentle art of not doing." For example, I learned that onions do not need to be monitored continuously in order to achieve their wonderful golden-brown color and sweet taste. That process is accomplished as long as they remain in contact with the surface of a hot pan for a given length of time. The tendency of cooks is to want to toss food around as soon as it hits the hot surface of the pan, but they should simply leave the food alone for a period of time. Though simple, this idea is based on an appreciation for ingredients and basic techniques.

Campbell learned this valuable lesson early in his career when a chef observed him preparing a dish flavored with mint. His technique was flawless, with a neat pile of finely sliced herbs ready to be folded into the dish. The chef paused and asked him if he had actually tasted the mint. Although Campbell automatically responded that he had, the chef persisted and had him place a bit of the herb in his mouth. Campbell later admitted that this was the first time he had really experienced the full impact of that ingredient. As if following the advice of Carlo Petrini, Cam[pbell] took the time to enjoy the moment. It is this progressive education that has taken him from a remote region of Scotland to the American Midwest and perhaps back again to the simple roots of his childhood, where he first developed a fundamental relationship with food and cooking. The essence of this bond is reflected in the following comment: "Get me a scallop and let me sauté it and poach it, and let me just eat it with the broth that comes off it. The goodness is available in the fish itself" (Campbell 2003).

Taking the time to learn about and savor good, simple food is at the heart of the culinary lessons taught by Angus Campbell, as well as Eugene Walter and Richard Olney. Campbell insists that culinary skills must be augmented by extended travel in order to fully immerse oneself in foreign cultures. In addition to enjoying a glass of local wine with the regional cuisine, we also need to meet the people and learn from them. Once we take the time to appreciate these two intertwined activities—cooking and eating—a new world of experiences will opens itself up to us.

References

Campbell, Angus. 2003. Personal interview with author. September 21.

Cary, T. 2005. "The Greater Grand Rapids Food Systems Council." Grand Rapids, MI, The Greater Grand Rapids Food Systems Council. Accessed June 16, at http://www.foodshed.net.

"Cooking with Angus Campbell: About Angus." 2004. Grand Rapids, Michigan, United States, Grand Rapids Community College. Accessed September 6, at http://web.grcc.cc.mi.us/about_angus.html.

Farr, S. Saylor. 1983. *More Than Moonshine: Appalachian Recipes and Recollections*. Pittsburgh, Pa: University of Pittsburgh Press.

"The Internet Guide to Scotland: The Isle of Lewis, Western Isles Tourism Board." 2002–2003. Accessed on September 19, 2004, at http://www.culturehebrides.com.

"Isle of Lewis." 2005. Accessed on March 7, at http://www.isle-of-lewis.com.

Rick, Deann, and Lanie Bayless

Promoting Flavor and the Appreciation of an Authentic Cuisine

About a month into my life in Oxford (I was a corporate swine for ten years in Atlanta before moving to Oxford, Mississippi, in 1995), I came across an article in *USA Today* about Rick Bayless. The article described Bayless' annual trips to Mexico with his staff, spending weeks eating, studying and talking and reading about regional native cuisine. A light bulb went on in my head even before I read the article's closing quote from Bayless wherein he described his touring and tasting as a form of culinary anthropology. I began to think about the South in those same terms.
—John T. Edge, Culinary Historians of Chicago

RICK BAYLESS FITS EASILY into the persona of a contemporary celebrity chef. He appears to be at the opposite end of the culinary spectrum of, say, Mama Dip. However, even though Bayless is suave, intense, and obviously knowledgeable, he shares a passion for authenticity and excellence with his counterpart in Chapel Hill.

The restaurants Bayless and his wife, Deann, opened have received national recognition. He won the James Beard Award for National Chef of the Year in 1995, and their cookbook, *Rick Bayless's Mexican Kitchen* (1996), was selected as the Julia Child/IACP Cookbook of the Year. Finally, Chef Bayless's PBS series, which has aired for several years, has also won critical acclaim. Bayless, however, has made substantial contributions in a number of other areas related to his work as a chef. He has a special talent for educating people about food by presenting it in a rich and sensual cultural context.

Bayless grew up in Oklahoma City, Oklahoma, amid a family of restaurateurs who specialized in barbecue. As he has stated, "My family has a long and proud history in the food business" (Bayless and Bayless 2004). His father established the Hickory House barbecue one year before Rick's birth (Bayless and Bayless 2004). According to Bayless, the family set a standard for local cuisine: "People would have their big, festive occasions. They would hire us to come and cater for them" (Bayless 2003). The eatery lasted for thirty-seven years.

While learning about the restaurant business, Bayless was also developing an appreciation for local cuisines. He saw the family business as contributing to the local culture, which influenced him when he later visited Mexico and experienced the uniqueness of each of its states.

Despite growing up with the foodservice business in his blood, Bayless turned away from it for a period of time. He studied Spanish and Latin American culture in undergraduate school (Bayless 2003), later pursuing a doctorate in anthropological linguistics at the University of Michigan. However, the academic life did not appeal to Bayless. He felt more alive in coffee shops and "places where there was a lot of activity." At the time he decided to return to food and "apply all the techniques that I learned in graduate school to studying Mexican food" (Bayless 2003). In 1978 and 1979 Bayless utilized his knowledge of Mexican culture and food in his role as host of the PBS series *Cooking Mexican* (Bayless 2003).

After the series ended, Bayless and his wife traveled to Mexico to study its food and culture. Over a period of six years, they visited every state in Mexico. It was from marketplace cooks at their stalls that

Bayless learned firsthand about Mexican cooking. He and Deann also participated in fiestas and frequented traditional family restaurants, where they would talk to the locals about Mexican food.

Given his background as an anthropologist, Bayless was able to obtain valuable information about people and places and the foods associated with them. Bayless insists that one needs to have some prior knowledge before conducting an interview about local foods. "[Y]ou don't say, how do you make that? That always elicits a response that is very shallow" (Bayless 2003). Instead he would ask about a particular ingredient included in a dish or pose a controversial question in order to stimulate discussion.

These experiences served as the basis for the education about Mexican food and culture that Bayless and his wife received. The research in which they engaged was that of anthropologists who live with people of another culture and participate in their daily lives—not unlike the experiences of Julia and Paul Child in Paris or Elizabeth David in Cairo. These group experiences have permitted Bayless to speak of Mexican food and culture from a very personal and intimate angle. Like Elizabeth David, Bayless is able to provide vivid descriptions of the people and places that inspire Mexican cuisine.

Upon their return to the United States, Bayless and his wife opened Frontera Grill at 445 North Clark Street. Several years later they opened an elegant Mexican restaurant called Topolobampo adjacent to Frontera. Topolobampo is considered to be one of only a handful of fine-dining restaurants featuring Mexican cuisine (Chefs Biography 2004).

It was thanks to the intimate knowledge gained as a result of years spent in Mexico that Bayless and his wife collaborated on *Authentic Mexican: Regional Cooking from the Heart of Mexico* (Bayless 1987). Unlike many cookbooks that simply focus on recipes and techniques, it combines culinary information with the culture that discovered and created it. It represents an effort as intense and prolonged as Julia Child's investment of time and energy in *Mastering the Art of French Cooking* (Child et al. 1961).

Bayless and his wife had traveled thousands of miles through Mexico, much of which was aboard buses and other forms of public transportation. By placing themselves so close to native culture, they stepped outside what is commonly referred to as the tourist bubble, the tendency of tourists to re-create or seek out familiar aspects of their own culture when traveling in foreign countries. Relinquishing this protective buffer is not as easy as it sounds. Bayless later commented on the unsettling nature of his initial introduction to authentic Mexican food. Like many Americans, he had grown accustomed to an Americanized version of Mexican food that he considered authentic. Bayless has noted that many people who travel internationally feel this discomfort "and . . . return home, a little more worldly-wise, to report with disappointment (and a little pride) that Mexican food down at Pablo's, say, is better than anything you can find in Mexico" (1987). By exposing this dilemma, however, he asks us to reconsider what it is like to experience authentic food—and perhaps even authentic culture—in foreign countries we choose to visit. In other words, when we dine at our favorite Mexican restaurant back home, we can enjoy the food while at the same time distinguishing between what is and is not authentic cuisine.

Bayless's book on Mexican cooking introduces the reader to the rich and varied food culture of Mexico. The book is filled with sensuous descriptions such as the following passage about mole poblano: "[N]atives' mouths water to visions of a dark, complex sauce made of dried chiles, nuts, seeds, flavoring vegetables, spices and, yes, a bit of chocolate" (Bayless 1987, 194) Like the writings of John T. Edge, the book is based on a sound historical foundation. Thus, when we read about the sweetness of cloves and cinnamon, we are reminded of an earlier passage on the Spanish and their introduction of these products to Mexico. Similarly, the Spanish preference for sweetness was partly inspired by their occupation by the Moors for eight centuries. The reader senses the complexities of Mexican cuisine and how they are reflected in contemporary Mexican culture.

New Pi

Creating Culture in a Local Market

National organic standards were put into effect in 2002.
Since then, controversy has been heating up over artificial
substances in certified organic products. It has now come
to a full-fledged fight.
—Jenifer Angerer, "Get Synthetics Out of Organics"

The term "food cooperative" frequently evokes images of small storefront operations staffed by volunteers, makeshift equipment, and granola spilled onto well-worn floors. That is certainly not the case with respect to the New Pioneer coopoerative (New Pi to its members and friends) in Iowa City and Coralville, Iowa, begun in 1970 as a food cooperative similar to that founded by Patti Zwick and her friends in Quincy, Illinois. As membership increased, the cooperative evolved into a storefront operation. The products offered at the store also multiplied over the years to include fresh meats, produce, and wines. This expansion was not without controversy, however, as founding members questioned the place of these products in an organization that was dedicated to wholesome foods. The discussion continues to this day.

New services were also offered, including a credit union. Members used the bulletin board to advertise goods and services, such as therapeutic massage and nutritional counseling. Having weathered a significant financial crisis, the new store now offers an espresso bar, freshly baked European-style breads, a deli, an extensive wine list, and even cooking classes. For example, Chad Clark, a staff member of the co-op, frequently offers pizza baking lessons.

There is a common thread uniting the food-buying club and the highly successful cooperative, with its multimillion-dollar budget and thousands of members. Both organizations provide a way for people to unite around a shared interest in food and food issues. For each of these groups, moreover, there is a sense of belonging to a larger entity and a spirit of camaraderie among its members. It's definitely not the same as dodging carts at the local superstore.

The narrow aisles invite conversation and permit a lively exchange of views on a particular product.

Seed Savers Exchange

Inspiring Flavor through the Preservation of Heritage

Our organization is saving the world's diverse, but endangered, garden heritage for future generations by building a network of people committed to collecting, conserving and sharing *heirloom seeds* and plants, while educating people about the value of genetic and cultural diversity.
—Seed Savers Exchange 2005

Rick Bayless, Susan Spicer, and other chefs consistently emphasize the importance of fresh ingredients. They also expand the range of their menus by utilizing many interesting foods not typically available in grocery stores and supermarkets. One interesting way to discover new flavors is through the use of heirloom foods. Heirloom plants are defined as "any garden plant that has a history of being passed down within a family, just like pieces of heirloom jewelry or furniture" (Seed Savers Exchange 2005).

One organization that promotes the preservation of heirloom foods is Seed Savers Exchange, located in Decorah, Iowa. According to its Web site, "Seed Savers Exchange was founded in 1975 by Diane and Kent Whealy, after her terminally-ill grandfather gave them the seeds of two garden plants, Grandpa Ott's Morning Glory and German Pink Tomato, that his parents brought from Bavaria when they immigrated to St. Lucas, Iowa in the 1870s" (Seed Savers Exchange 2005). They subsequently developed a membership organization around the preservation and use of heirloom plants. By promoting the propagation of vegetables such as Chrysalis purple garlic and the Cherokee Purple tomato, members of Seed Savers Exchange have access to an interesting array of different flavors. They also contribute to the genetic diversity of the planet.

The Frontera Farmer Foundation

Promoting Sustainable and Artisanal Cuisine

The small family farms that dot the Midwestern landscape and
provide food to local businesses are struggling to maintain

viability among today's big agri-giants. Yet it's these farms that
produce some of the freshest, highest-quality produce available
to Chicago-area restaurants. With the help of the Frontera Farmer
Foundation—started by Frontera Grill and Topolobamop founders
Rick and Deann Bayless—these farms are beginning to thrive.
—National Restaurant Association,
"Restaurant Neighbor Award 2005 Finalist"

In addition to managing their restaurants and an ambitious publishing and production schedule, Rick and Deann Bayless have contributed to the cuisine of their home community of Chicago, Illinois,
through the establishment of The Frontera Farmer Foundation. The
beliefs of the foundation, as stated on their Web site, are straightforward and echo those of Slow Food: "Small, local farms promote
biodiversity by planting a wide range of produce, are more likely to
operate using organic practices, and add immeasurably to the fabric
of their communities by their civic commitments, interactions with
restaurant chefs and presence at farmers' markets" (The Frontera
Farmer Foundation 2004).

The foundation was established when an area producer of organic tomatoes who needed freezers to store excess inventory approached his customer, Frontera Grill, for financial assistance (Slama
2003). Frontera provided the financing, and the producer paid off
the loan with a regular supply of tomatoes, which actually tasted
better after being frozen. The experience motivated Bayless and
his managers to create a foundation to support local organic and
artisanal producers of foods.

Since its inception in 2003, the foundation has sponsored a variety of small-scale initiatives, including the creation of "a mobile
vending cart for selling sandwiches at farmers' markets as a way
of introducing people to the flavor of local ranchers' and farmers'

products." The foundation gives Bayless and his wife the opportunity to educate people about different, often neglected, foods and to add to the quality of food culture in a major metropolitan region. Bayless has emphasized the importance of basing a great cuisine on the use of quality local ingredients (Howard 2005).

Bayless's support for locally produced ingredients expanded to the national level when he headed up the Chef's Collaborative, a network that encourages sustainable food production (Slama 2003). The organization, founded in 1993, supports the following: (1) artisanal producers, many of whom are preserving valuable traditions; (2) local growers, who enrich our communities by providing our restaurants and farmers' markets with distinctive, delicious, seasonal produce; (3) all who work toward sustainable agriculture and aquaculture, humane animal husbandry, and well-managed fisheries; (4) conservation practices that lessen our impact on the environment (Chef's Collaborative 2005). Chefs who belong to the organization emphasize the need for close, personal links with their suppliers. This has helped chefs maintain a high level of quality in their foods. Reliance on small, artisanal producers has also enabled chefs such as Susan Spicer to gain access to new products that she can feature on her menu (Chef's Collaborative 2005).

Bayless's intertwining of food and culture reflects a unique culinary language. He wants food to "talk to people" (Bayless 2003). He gives credit to chefs who are willing to experiment and force people to look at traditional foods in new ways. Creativity, however, must be grounded in a more traditional base. It is only the latter that is capable of preserving a sense of regional identity.

Just as Julia Child traveled extensively earlier in her career and continued to learn about food and culture throughout her life, Bayless returns to Mexico every year, accompanied by a number of his restaurant staff. While in Mexico, Bayless directs individual research into marketplaces and other public spaces where food is sold and shared. Each individual is given an assignment, with the group later returning to compare their experiences, prepare food, and share it communally.

The sensuality of Bayless's writing is also reflected in his approach to learning how to cook. In a manner reminiscent of Slow Food advocates, he emphasizes the need for a successful cook to value good flavor. He criticizes the tendency of many culinary schools to emphasize technique, which he sees as merely a path to good flavor: "Technique is only an instrument to achieve certain flavors, but if you've never talked about flavor, you have no idea. It's like going down a path and having no idea where you're headed; you just get lost" (Bayless 2003).

Bayless's emphasis on flavor over technique also influences the way he trains his restaurant staff. A contemporary chef might also engage in anthropological research in Mexico or another foreign culture. However, how likely is it that this same chef would have a large number of staff with him to help with this research? The expense would clearly be prohibitive for most food service operations. It is more likely that the chef would conduct his own research, create a menu, and train his staff to prepare and present the food. When Bayless takes restaurant staff with him, he accomplishes more than culinary training. He creates a web of talent and passion within his organization. To a great extent, this process also enhances employee satisfaction with their work.

The rich cultural and gastronomic information Bayless and his wife have continued to amass has inspired a new series of PBS broadcasts. *Mexico, One Plate at a Time with Rick Bayless* entered its third season in September 2004. This series and its accompanying books have proven extremely popular. However, they are not just entertaining and cover far more than Mexican food and cookery.

Mexico, One Plate at a Time with Rick Bayless is colorful and noisy. Although vivid images of foods and sound effects are present throughout the broadcasts, the viewer is also introduced to social elements of Mexican culture as a backdrop to the food. In one early broadcast entitled "Ceviche in the Limelight" (Bayless 2001), he prepares ceviche on the beach. The background sounds include gulls and the roar of surf. In addition to presenting the straightforward recipe, Bayless suggests the historical antecedent for the dish as a form of food preservation. The preparation of ceviche thus permits him to segue into an explanation of the lime's role in this particular dish as well as in Mexican cuisine as a whole: "Lime and spicy chilies are the salt and pepper of Mexico" (Bayless 2001). He next compares the lemon criollo (key lime) with the Persian lime with which American cooks are more familiar. Bayless drives home his point by emphasizing the intense sensory experience of the key lime—a combination of strong aroma and sharp taste. Finally, he describes the combination of flavors in Mexican food and how lime juice helps create that perfect balance.

Bayless also takes the time to point out misconceptions Americans have regarding Mexican food. For example, in another episode he quietly suggests that we should not think of all Mexican food as being coated with a heavy layer of cheese. He then compares a number of Mexican dishes, such as mojo and escabeche, to Mediterranean foods—both being light, simple, and flavorful. All of this gastronomic and cultural information enables viewers to expand their culinary repertoire while at the same time experiencing the complexity of Mexican cultural life.

While remaining grounded in traditional Mexican cuisine, Bayless also seizes every opportunity to add new dimensions to traditional foods. In the case of ceviche, for example, he suggests using salmon, which can be found in most American supermarkets. He even adjusts the acid marinade by including orange juice. The inventive cook is thus presented with a novel way of interpreting a traditional dish through an understanding of how it differs from tradition. This form of culinary education is far removed from those celebrity chefs who utilize a "just follow the directions" approach to culinary education.

Bayless, his wife, and their daughter Lanie have embarked on yet another publishing project called *Rick and Lanie's Excellent Kitchen Adventures: Recipes and Stories* (Bayless and Bayless 2004). Here they expand their focus to include foods from France, Morocco, and

Thailand. The book also adds another dimension by demonstrating how two cooks—veteran chef and novice—experience the same recipes (Chefs Biography 2004). Father and daughter prepare the same dishes and then compare notes. They also share their impressions of the different cultures they visit, thus creating an interesting dialogue. For example, while Bayless describes a beautiful sky over the ruins of Monte Alban and the Oaxaca valley, Lanie carps about the bumpy ride and the heat. While Bayless sees the beautiful arrangements of food in the market as a reflection of "the people's deep-seated respect for their food," Lanie sees them as "not organized like at the Jewel or Dominick's grocery story. And—let me be honest here—some of it doesn't smell all that great. Especially the d-r-i-e-d f-i-s-h" (Bayless and Bayless 2004, 15). Lanie's occasionally irreverent tone reflects the alternating amusement and revulsion that young people experience whenever they consider the role of tradition in their lives.

Bayless also discusses the role of tradition and traditional foods: "I'm a firm believer in special food served on special plates for special days. This intention to create something meaningful helps us break the dulling sameness of everyday, so we can completely focus on the 'here and now.' Especially the people in our here-and-now" (Bayless and Bayless 2004). The interaction between father and daughter revolves around discovery and rediscovery, tradition versus innovation. The reader cannot help but think that the Bayless tradition will be carried forward by Lanie, assuming she chooses this path for herself. If so, the challenge will be to discover what constitutes her own true expression.

References

Bayless, R. 1987. *Authentic Mexican: Regional Cooking from the Heart of Mexico.* New York: William Morrow.

Bayless, R. 2001. "Ceviche in the Limelight." Mexico, One Plate at a Time with Rick Bayless. PBS.

Bayless, R. 2003. Interview with author. Frontera Grill, Chicago, Ill. July 11.

Bayless, R., and L. Bayless. 2004. *Rick And Lanie's Excellent Kitchen Adventures: Recipes and Stories.* New York: Stewart, Tabori & Chang.

Chef's Biography. 2004. "Chef Rick Bayless Biography." Accessed on December 22, at http://www.starchefs.com/chefs/rbayless/html/biography.shtml.

Chef's Collaborative. 2005. "Partners in Local, Artisanal and Sustainable Cuisine." Accessed on June 17, at http://www.chefscollaborative.org.

Child, J., et al. 1961. *Mastering the Art of French Cooking.* New York: Alfred A. Knopf.

Culinary Historians of Chicago. 2001. "Grits and Greens Highlights." Accessed on December 17, 2004, at http://www.culinaryhistorians.org/news/gnghigh.htm.

Frontera. 2004. "Meet Rick Bayless." Accessed at http://www.fronterakitchens.com/rickbayless/bio.html.

The Frontera Farmer Foundation. 2004. Accessed on December 22, at http://www.fonterakitchens.com/restaurants/foundation.

Howard, D. 2005. "From Farms to Five Stars." Accessed on January 12, at http://www.motherearthnews.com/library/2003_october_november/from_farms_to_five_stars.

Seed Savers Exchange. 2005. Accessed on June 21, at http://www.seedsavers.org/Home.asp.

Slama, J. 2003. "Do Bet the Farm." Conscious Choice. Accessed on June 17, 2005, at http://www.consciouschoice.com/2003/cc1609/rickbayless1609.html. .

Father Dominic Garramone, O.S.B.

Food and Cooking as an Expression of Spirituality

> One of my personal goals as a priest is to help people
> develop a "domestic spirituality" based on their ordinary
> lives, so that the kitchen is seen as a sacred space, and
> the home can be the locus of holiness just as much as a
> sanctuary of the church.
> —Matt Andrew, "Breaking Bread with Father Dominic"

THE CITIES OF LA SALLE and Peru, Illinois, are situated along a rural stretch of the Illinois River north of Peoria. Together they represent a community that is the home of St. Bede Abbey, hardly a place one would associate with an accomplished baker who has had his own public television series. This, however, is the home of Father Dominic Garramone, aka Papa Dom, who is passionate about many things—including baking.

St. Bede Abbey has existed in the La Salle/Peru area since the nineteenth century. It is also the home of Saint Bede Academy, a Catholic preparatory school for young men and women established in 1891. The campus buildings and monastery are located on one hundred acres of woodland, but the monastic community also owns and manages nearly a thousand acres of farmland that include over twelve hundred apple trees. In fact, St. Bede cider has taken top honors at the Illinois Specialty Growers Convention, and honey from the abbey's apiary is in demand throughout the Illinois Valley (Andrew 2004).

The monastery is home to thirty-five Benedictine monks who have taken a vow of stability to remain at St. Bede Abbey for the remainder of their lives. With the assistance of the lay community, the monks are actively involved in the administration of the academy, including serving on the faculty (Andrew 2004).

At St. Bede Father Garramone teaches religion, directs the theater, and bakes for students, his peers, and even for the local community. For example, as part of a recent fund-raising event, a pizza dinner for eight prepared by Father Garramone was auctioned off for a thousand dollars. The breads and pizzas are prepared in a modest kitchen containing old but well-maintained equipment. Many of the tools he uses were handmade by his father.

Father Garramone's lessons about bread are typically aimed at viewers who are amateurs, or Bread Heads, as described by his sister (Garramone 2001). He is careful to explain that his use of this term does not imply a lack of knowledge but simply that the love of this activity is important to many nonprofessionals.

In his work Father Garramone stresses the connection between baking and the challenges of contemporary life. He quietly suggests that baking bread is a way to slow down, forcing us to "put the brakes on our hectic lives. . . . It's just not possible to be in a hurry when you're waiting for dough to rise" (Cafazzo 2000). While that advice may not sit well with the "bolt and dash generation," Father Garramone's philosophy asks us to consider why our contemporary lifestyles emphasize short-term goals.

This running social commentary, combined with Father Garramone's quick wit, represents an important element of his work. For him, baking bread is a way to bring people together. He illustrates his point by using an office setting as an example. If you bring a batch of cookies to work, people will take one and return to their respective work stations. However, if you substitute a loaf of warm bread, people will frequently interact while they eat the bread. For Father Garramone, the processes of baking and eating both bring people together—often from very different social strata. This occurred when he took time out from a publicity tour in Texas to bake with a group of adolescent offenders in a high-security facility run by the Texas Youth Commission (Kever 2000). Dressed in a black hooded monk's habit and his trademark Converse sneakers, Father Garramone mixed bread lore with spirituality in the company of ten juveniles, some of whom were serving time for capital murder. Scenes such as this illustrate what Father Garramone's television show presents to viewers: a realistic portrait of an engaged cleric living in the twenty-first century.

Like other individuals who write about food and teach the craft of cooking, Father Garramone also provides his viewers and readers with an opportunity to consider the nature of the process according to which good food is created. The bread produced by hand is not the same each time, a reminder that people are also imperfect. Bread machines create a homogenized product: "There is a kind of sameness to bread machine bread" (Keeler 2001). Not only does Father Garramone demonstrate his love for the craft of baking, he also stresses the connection between baking and spirituality. After all, Father Garramone is, first and foremost, a Benedictine monk and priest (Andrew 2004). He is emphatic in explaining that his religious vocation shapes him as a baker, not vice versa. Likewise, it is his dedication to a vocation in the Benedictine order, not his avocation as a baker, that serves as the basis for his PBS show. This emphasis on spirituality differentiates Father Garramone from many other individuals who teach us about food. How many "self-anointed" baking gurus with television programs encourage us to "bake and be blessed" (Garramone 2002) or to relax because bread is always forgiving (Cafazzo 2000)?

Father Garramone was born and raised in Peoria, Illinois. In a fashion reminiscent of James Beard's family, the Garramones preserved baking traditions from different segments of their extended families. For example, his mother, Mary, learned how to make bread called povitica—with a filling of honey, walnuts, and cinnamon—from her Austrian ancestors. She and Grandma Tootsie were excellent bakers and included the children in their baking activities. Father Garramone emphasizes that baking was the norm in the Garramone household (Hines-Brigger 2003). His siblings all developed an appreciation for the craft of cooking and baking.

It was in elementary school that Father Garramone experienced his first significant encounter with the craft of baking. As a fifth grader at the Sacred Heart School in Peoria, he was asked to create something French for his class. He discussed the assignment with his mother, who suggested that he bake French bread.

Although Father Garramone no longer remembers the actual process of baking the French bread with his mother, he vividly recalls bringing it to school with a tub of unsalted butter and a jar of homemade apricot preserves. He also brought along his mother's best bread knife and a cutting board. The success of his baking experiment was evidenced by a few crumbs, a matted pad of butter, and a jar with a small amount of residue at the bottom.

For Father Garramone the payoff resided in the fact that he had created something that people genuinely appreciated and was able to experience what it was like to nourish others with the gift of food. He related his feelings about the project in our interview: "It just made me feel better about the whole project. It made me feel like I had achieved something really special that people liked, and perhaps no one else [in the class] could have done." The importance of contributing to the well-being of others through baking and similar activities remains at the core of Father Garramone's life.

In high school Father Garramone became active in theater, helping to produce the musical *Fiddler on the Roof* as well as other theatrical events. All the while he continued to conduct food research, such as how to make challah—special bread eaten by Jews during the Sabbath and religious holidays—and shared it with the rest of the cast.

Cooking with Fire in Public

The Bake Ovens of Dufferin Grove Park

If you want to bake your own bread, you can come after 3 P.M. on Thursdays and use the residual heat left from the farmers' market baking. If you want to learn how we bake the bread, you're welcome to come and watch anytime on Thursdays between 8 A.M. and 2 P.M. You can also get free sourdough starter from us to take home. But don't try to chat much with the bakers; they need to concentrate on their work. And don't ask about workshops or lessons—there won't be any. It's not a school. But if you want to watch and learn that way, you're welcome.
—Friends of Dufferin Grove Park 2005

In 1993 a small group of Toronto residents calling themselves the Friends of Dufferin Grove Park created a project named "The Big Backyard" in which they cooked over campfires together with children who frequented the park. This project was later expanded to include a wood-fired brick oven in which they baked bread (Friends of Dufferin Grove Park 2005b). Several years later another oven was added. The ovens and their accompanying smoke reflect Father Dominic Garramone's emphasis on the ability of bread to bring people together.

Dufferin Grove Park, in downtown Toronto, occupies approximately two city blocks. The brick ovens are situated near a basketball court and an ice rink. The location of the ovens draws people to them. When the ovens are in use, it is not unusual for total strangers to stop and inquire about what is being baked. A virtual community has thus arisen around the ovens.

A variety of seasonal activities have evolved as part of the culture associated with these ovens. During the summer there are community dinners scheduled on Fridays. Participants use produce from the local farmers' market, and the Bake Ovens are used to prepare foods. A program called Pizza in the Park occurs several days each week, where children make their own pizzas. The park staff provide the basic ingredients and children are encouraged to bring special toppings. In addition to a regular Saturday-morning bake sale, the ovens have been used during fund-raisers. Schools have even organized field trips to the ovens so that students can learn how to bake pizzas.

What makes these ovens so special is that they bring people together to share food—which is not necessarily healthier or better-tasting. The critical element is the convivial atmosphere created by drawing together people from the local community.

When he entered college, baking and cooking became more of a practical skill for Father Garramone. A kitchenette in the dormitory was rarely used and there was no food service on Sunday evenings. Father Garramone would bake bread on Sundays, with friends contributing cheese and other foods for their evening meal. On one occasion the entire floor held a spaghetti party, with Father Garramone contributing twenty-six loaves of bread. Baking became a source of strength similar to that which helped James Beard through economically stressful times. Even more, it became part of Father Garramone's identity.

Father Garramone's baking skills were developed gradually. Like Eugene Walter, he was self-taught. He was influenced by James Beard's book on bread, which his mother used as a reference. He also watched a television series called *The Galloping Gourmet* and utilized a book on breads by Bernard Clayton. He began to develop an appreciation for the cultural underpinnings associated with food and cooking, which surfaces again and again in his television programs. For example, in one episode (Andrew 1999), he entices viewers with festive breads such as challah and potivica, an Austrian specialty made by his family for generations. His recipes are also peppered with stories of the different breads and their importance to the people who bake and eat them.

Father Garramone's road to the monastic life was a long one. He had first experienced a calling during high school. This, however, was a difficult topic to make public at that age. While Dominic was still in high school, Father Placid Hatfield, O.S.B., accompanied him to the abbey in Peru, Illinois, for a visit (Hines-Brigger 2003). After a second visit, Dominic was certain this was the place for him. Instead of entering the seminary, Father Garramone enrolled at Illinois Wesleyan University, where he studied theater. He did so to prove that his calling was not simply the result of having been deeply immersed in the Catholic culture as a child (Hines-Brigger 2003). In 1981 Father Garramone began a thirty-day novena to St. Joseph (Garramone 2003). At the end of the novena, he visited St. Bede's Abbey and expressed his intention to join the religious community. When he applied, the abbot told Father Garramone that their academy needed a drama teacher and theater manager. As a result, Father Garramone entered Immaculate Heart of Mary Seminary, where he continued to work in the theater while pursuing his religious studies. Father Garramone entered the monastery in 1983 and took his solemn vows in 1989 (Hines-Brigger 2003).

Father Garramone's talent for baking became important to all of the abbey's members. Explaining that the monastic life favors the server, he recalled in an interview how being a baker became another form of service: "I've been very inspired by just the fact that I live with 30 hungry bachelors, you know, who cannot get enough bread or cookies."

As Father Garramone's reputation as a baker became known throughout the abbey community, his fellow monks and priests would often request that he bake particular types of bread that reminded them of home. Father Garramone has characterized this aspect of life in the monastery as providing him with a built-in focus group about breads: "The monks have a wide range of backgrounds, coming from different states and countries, and all have had varied food experiences" (Heath 2001). He has tested recipes on his fellow monks, who gladly provide feedback. For example, when a batch of pumpernickel bread ended up with the texture appropriate for a doorstop, one of his fellow monks gently suggested that it simply needed some additional air (Heath 2001). With so many different backgrounds to draw upon, Father Garramone soon developed a repertoire of over fifty different recipes for bread.

Father Garramone had the opportunity to attend an institute in Colorado for growing and using herbs, where he was introduced to a book by Shandor and Gaea Weis entitled *Growing & Using Healing Herbs* (1985). This book, as well as Phyllis Shaudys's *Pleasure of Herbs* (1986), inspired Father Garramone to start an herb garden in the monastery. Having done so, he needed to discover ways in which the herbs could be used. His breads served as the perfect vehicle for this purpose. One of his early experiences involving the use of fresh herbs in bread occurred one Thanksgiving. Father Garramone had intended to use fresh sage in the turkey stuffing. After harvesting the fresh herbs, he returned to discover that the cooks had already made the stuffing and flavored it with canned sage from the supermarket. Though disappointed, Father Garramone decided to create a whole wheat bread with the flavors associated with stuffing. He sautéed onions and added them to the dough along with the herbs. The result was bread that had the flavor of stuffing and made excellent cold turkey sandwiches. As a result of such experiments, Father Garramone soon accumulated over thirty new recipes.

An outgrowth of Father Garramone's herb production has been the establishment of Thursdays as pizza night. Father Ronald, a huge fan of pizza, was uncomfortable with making crusts from scratch. He asked Father Garramone to help make dough, and they began to bake large quantities on sheet pans. They then obtained a pizza stone and Father Garramone began to add fresh herbs to the dough in addition to the sauce. Making pizza has now become a fixture at both the academy and the monastery. It is an integral component of the abbey's "haustus" night, in which, in addition to "Papa Dom's" homemade pizza, members of the community share food and conversation over board games and cards.

Father Garramone clearly demonstrates both his love of baking and his love of his fellow man. Thursday evenings in the academy kitchen is one place where his love for others is expressed through his baking. On one Thursday evening when I visited him, Father Garramone encouraged me to help with the preparation of pizzas for the monastic community. We were joined by several students who "just" happened to stop by when they heard that pizza was on the menu. Shortly thereafter I made the acquaintance of an alumna, who drove from the northern suburbs of Chicago to introduce her fiancée to Father Garramone.

During the evening, we shared stories and told jokes in the quiet kitchen. Father Garramone occasionally provided me with suggestions as to how I could improve my technique of tossing the pizza dough. There was comfort in our shared work, and soon we dispatched pizzas to the monks' card game and turned to the task of making our own. Each person had a favorite topping for his or her pizza and related different stories about baking pizza in the same kitchen. As we broke bread together, I was reminded of one of Father Garramone's favorite expressions. He often emphasizes that the English word "companion" is based on the Latin for "with bread." We parted company that evening as friends.

Father Garramone even uses the process of baking pizza as a way to develop a sense of rapport with his students, especially those who are somewhat isolated from their peers in the academy. Father Garramone frequently encourages them to join him, together with their friends, to bake pizza over the weekend.

While Father Garramone's baking skills continued to develop, his calling to the faith took a different turn when he decided to become a priest. He emphasizes that this different calling originated with other people—especially his students, who encouraged him to follow this path (Hines-Brigger 2003). He was ordained in 1992 and celebrated his first mass at St. Bede Abbey's chapel.

The television debut of *Breaking Bread with Father Dominic* was the result of a friend from elementary school contacting station KETC, the PBS station in St. Louis, Missouri (Keeler 2001), and describing Father Garramone's work. The producers expressed an interest and came to watch him teach. According to Father Garramone, the producers came on a day that he was teaching a freshman religion class about the multiplication of the loaves. In his lecture, he conducted an exercise he called "What Kind of Bread Shall We Be?," with discussion centering on different kinds of bread and how they symbolize different kinds of Christian ministry (Hines-Brigger, 2003). This was the same exercise he conducted with a group of youths in a detention facility in Texas.

At the conclusion of the class, Father Garramone was offered a television show. Although he was initially reluctant, after discussing the matter with the abbot, both decided that the show would provide an opportunity to present a positive, realistic portrayal of a Catholic monk. Father Garramone and the producers agreed that he would be depicted as a monk and priest who bakes, not as a baker who happens to belong to a religious order. During an interview with National Public Radio host Renee Montagne, Father Garramone emphasized that his religious vocation is "what makes the program what it is. The appeal is that here's a guy who thinks that something else is more important" (Montagne 2002). Baking is thus used as a way to illuminate spirituality in our everyday lives and to encourage viewers to look for spirituality in their own lives: "'The Rule of Saint Benedict says that monks are to treat the tools of the monastery with the same reverence as for the sacred vessels of the altar,' says Father Dominic. 'He clearly saw that the abbey kitchen, the garden and the workshop could be sacred spaces, too. We need to reclaim that kind of vision for every home'" (Andrew 2004).

The television series *Breaking Bread with Father Dominic* debuted in 1999. The show has aired in approximately one hundred markets. Over the course of three seasons Father Garramone has both entertained and instructed. Utilizing a wry sense of humor usually directed at himself, he opens up a world of different breads to viewers while emphasizing the need to come into close, physical contact with the dough. According to Father Garramone, the dough and the yeast contained within it is a living organism. It is through contact with this organism and the sense of making and sharing something as special as a warm loaf of bread that we can animate our lives.

From Jewish challah and Austrian povitica to Ethiopian amba-sha, Father Garramone has demonstrated how different cultures relate to bread. Over the course of three successive seasons he has encouraged viewers to take the time to bake their own bread and to appreciate the act itself. This process demands concentration in order to unify the senses. The physical act of handling the ingredients and kneading them into a smooth, elastic dough becomes a form of meditation. In fact, Father Garramone stresses getting one's hands into the dough and learning through touch. In an episode on the fundamentals of baking bread, he demonstrates how to determine when the dough has leavened enough by poking holes in it and comparing its texture with another ball of dough that has not risen at all.

During an interview with Renee Montagne (2002), Father Garramone was asked how he felt about being referred to as a star. He responded that "star is not a monk word" and suggested that the "host" was a better choice. I personally prefer "companion" to describe Father Garramone. I cannot think of a better person with whom to break bread.

References

Andrew, M. 2004. "Breaking Bread with Father Dominic." KETC, St. Louis, Mo. Accessed on August 4, at http://www.breaking-bread.com/about/about.htm.

Cafazzo, D. 2000. "Benedictine Baker with Books and a PBS Show." *News Tribune* [Tacoma, Wash.] November 15.

Friends of Dufferin Grove Park. 2005a. "Cooking with Fire in Public." Accessed on June 17, at http://dufferinpark.ca/oven/pdf/cookingwithfire.pdf.

Friends of Dufferin Grove Park. 2005b. "Our Community Bake Ovens and Food at the Park." Accessed on June 17, at http://www.dufferinpark.ca/oven/bakeover.html#abouttheovens.

Garramone, D. 2001. *More Breaking Bread.* KETC, St. Louis, Mo.

———. 2002. *Bake and Be Blessed: Bread Baking as a Metaphor for Spiritual Growth.* KETC, St. Louis, Mo.

———. 2003. Interview with author, St. Bede Abbey. June 14.

Heath, E. 2001. "Father Dominic Casts His Bread on TV Viewers." *Des Moines Register* February 21.

Hines-Brigger, S. 2003. "In the Kitchen with Father Dominic." *St. Anthony Messenger* 111: 30.

Keeler, J. 2001. "Good Things Come to Those Who Knead." *St. Petersburg Times* March 7.

Kever, J. 2000. "A Time of Knead: TV Monk Breaks Bread with Teens in Trouble." *Houston Chronicle* February 17.

Montagne, R. 2002. "Profile: Professional and Personal Lives Poles Apart." *Morning Edition* (NPR) August 5.

Shaudys, P. 1986. *Pleasure of Herbs: A Month-by-Month Guide to Growing, Using, and Enjoying Herbs.* Pownal, Vt.: Workman.

Weis, G., and S. Weis. 1985. *Growing & Using Healing Herbs.* Emmaus, Pa.: Rodale.

John T. Edge
and the Southern
Foodways Alliance

Narrative as a Way to Understand Food and Society

> While all around us the South is being transformed into one
> big strip mall, barbecue remains intransigent. It's our great
> cultural standard-bearer, the culinary rock of Gibraltar.
> —John T. Edge, "Memphis Specializes in Mutant
> Barbecue, Anything Southern"

I DROVE DOWN TO OXFORD, MISSISSIPPI, in order to interview John T. Edge, the director of the Southern Foodways Alliance (SFA). I spent several hours with Edge in his office, where we
discussed his background and work. At lunchtime he suggested we
drive a few miles south of Oxford and visit the Taylor Grocery and
Restaurant, which Edge had described in his book *Southern Belly:
The Ultimate Food Lover's Companion to the South* (2000). It was
exactly as he had described: not much to look at from the outside,
quiet, and a great place for fried catfish. I first heard about Edge on
National Public Radio, where he read a story taken from his book *A
Gracious Plenty: Recipes and Recollections from the American South*
(1999). It was about an old widower attempting to make a batch of

biscuits just like his wife had done so often in the past. This bitter-sweet story revealed special forms of knowledge and included lore of the kitchen. It was from this story and others like it that I developed the title and theme of my dissertation, "Great Cooks as Adult Learners: The Lore and Lure of the Kitchen" (2001).

Edge grew up in rural Georgia in the seventies. His hometown, Clinton, was a small community northeast of Macon. Despite its size, Clinton is a place with a strong sense of history. Edge's family home had served as the former residence of a Confederate general. In his introduction to *Georgia* (2001a). Edge describes Clinton as the place where he "learned the lessons that would later define my life" (13).

Edge's father bestowed an unusual gift on him in the form of a line of credit at a local barbecue joint called the Old Clinton Barbecue. The line of credit covered barbecue and Orange Crush. Edge recalled spending much of his youth traveling to and from this barbecue joint. He makes a special point of describing Mrs. Coulter, the proprietor's mother, who dished out "barbecue, coleslaw and Brunswick stew" (Edge 2003) to the patrons. This biographical approach illustrates an important aspect of Edge's writing: the food is always discussed in relation to the people who prepare and serve it, and descriptions invariably include social factors, such as race relations.

It was not simply his father's funding that sparked Edge's interest in food. His father often traveled to Atlanta in search of unusual condiments and ingredients and would try them out in the kitchen or on the grill. Edge has described his father as an adventuresome cook who frequently escorted him to diners and other small eateries where they could see their food actually being prepared before their eyes.

Before he began writing about food, Edge spent nearly nine years on the road as a salesman for a financial news service (Shriver 2000), later referring to himself as a "corporate swine" (Culinary Historians of Chicago 2001). He nevertheless followed his father's example by seeking out unusual places to eat. Over the course of many years, he began to develop taste knowledge, which he now combines with a wealth of stories about people and food.

It is these stories that animate Edge's descriptions of food. He even confessed the following to Noah Adams of National Public Radio: "Recipes bore me. But I believe that listening to the life stories of plain old good cooks can reveal insights about our society" (National Public Radio 2001). It is not sufficient to simply understand food. What is paramount is to appreciate the people who prepare and serve the food to us. Edge is not talking about celebrity chefs but rather the invisible hands that pass plates through kitchen windows in the "back of the house" or the anonymous individuals who dexterously set them before us. Edge believes that we must listen to their stories in order to fully understand these people.

Edge's narratives of people and food are spiked with a sense of irony and subtle humor. In *Apple Pie: An American Story* (2004a) he attempts to construct a "theory of gargantuan-size pies" (44), citing a time in early American history when pie ingredients were referred to as timber, a reference to construction. According to Edge, "Implicit was the acknowledgement that a sturdy crust filled with honest apples is a thing of substance best described in terms used by craftsmen" (45). He goes on to develop a story about the intertwining of architecture and pie that undergoes modification when his wife suggests that the process of creating huge pies could reflect a compulsion to engage in large-scale construction projects.

Edge then transitions into a description of a pie baker named Tootie Feagan. Describing her as a "Rockwellian grandmother," he sketches her education as a pie baker. Throughout his entire narrative, in a single sentence Edge captures the essence of Tootie's pies: "As I heft a buxom slice to my mouth and chomp down through a rich crust that does not so much shatter as flake apart" (47). By the time I had reached the end of the chapter, my mouth was watering. I paused, uncertain whether to continue writing or head for the kitchen and begin assembling tools and ingredients. Life is full of tough decisions.

Edge's humor has a mischievous aspect. Like the Native American trickster character, he intentionally shatters the complacent attitude that characterizes our relationship with cooking and eating traditions. For example, in an autobiographical essay entitled "Open House" (2004c) Edge describes his exploration of the "dark side" of public places where people eat together, such as taverns, coffeehouses, cafés. It begins with his initiation into a fraternity, including a 2 A.M. visit to a local diner where he "scarfed a platter of eggs and grits." The diner was, in his words, a late-night "holding tank" for young drunks. Rumor had it that it also served as a gathering place for the Klan. At the time, that aspect did not seem all that important to Edge and his university friends. He later admitted that "we just turned a deaf ear and ordered another cheeseburger. What right did we have to stir up the past?" However, it is precisely that aspect Edge emphasizes in the remainder of the essay as he explores the history of a hate crime with ties to the diner and its owner. As he tells his story, we are similarly challenged to dig into our own histories and replay those moments during which we turned a deaf ear. This trickster makes it difficult for us to forget.

Another illustration of Edge's talent for illuminating hidden aspects of our relationship with food occurs in his description of plains farming families who traveled from one ranch to another during the nineteenth century. While the men worked in the fields, "the wives would work indoors, shucking and boiling corn, frying chicken and baking pies" (Edge 2003). In a manner similar to Karen Hess, who pays homage to the African women of the South Carolina rice kitchens (1998), Edge pays tribute to these hard-working women. In another book (2004b) Edge credits African American women for helping to create fried chicken: "Perhaps it will suffice to observe that, in the eighteenth century—while cooking for (and sometimes under the direction of) white slaveholders—women of African descent honed a dish we now know as fried chicken." In line with Arlene Voski Avakian (1997), who views cooking as a source of power for women, Edge speculates that raising and preparing chickens for sale provided African American women a certain degree of self-reliance.

Edge's narrative illustrates the considerable effort he invests in developing an understanding of the rich historical and cultural aspects of food. His style of writing makes the text he creates both engaging and informative. He has suggested two ways to read books such as *Fried Chicken*. One is to "eat" your way through the book by utilizing the recipes he has furnished. The other is to explore modern social history through food.

Given his passion for food culture and his ability to ferret out interesting information about even the simplest items, it is not difficult to understand why Edge is the director of a group that describes itself as "a diverse bunch: cookbook authors and anthropologists, culinary historians and good home cooks, organic gardeners and barbecue pitmasters, food journalists and inquisitive eaters, nativeborn Southerners and outlanders too (Southern Foodways Alliance 2003).

The Southern Foodways Alliance (SFA) was created in 1999 as a collaborative venture involving fifty professionals who shared a common interest, namely, the foodways of the southern United States. A division of the Center for the Study of Southern Culture, the aim of the SFA is "to celebrate, preserve, promote, and nurture the traditional and developing diverse food cultures of the American South" (Southern Foodways Alliance 2000–2003).

Like the Slow Food movement, SFA strives to preserve the unique identity of a specific region's identity. Similarly, SFA routinely spearheads a number of different initiatives. One is to record the oral history of food in the South: "Our Oral History Initiative seeks to capture stories of Southerners who grow, create, serve, and consume food and drink" (Southern Foodways Alliance 2003d).

One ongoing SFA Oral History Initiative is the BBQ Oral History Project (Southern Foodways Alliance 2003b). Here SFA and Slow Food share a common belief in slowness: "When it comes to barbecue, change is accursed. Speed is anathema" (2003b). SFA emphasizes the importance of slowness in its description of the essential elements of barbecue, namely, "a time-intensive marriage of smoke, meat, sweat and sauce" (Southern Foodways Alliance 2003a).

Among the goals of the BBQ Oral History Project was the documenting of barbecue joints in and around Memphis, which was undertaken by Amy Evans and Joe York (Southern Foodways Alliance 2003c). One of the individuals interviewed was J. C. Hardaway. He had been cooking for fifty-nine years, "since the age of 19." His first experience with food was at the Hawkins Grill, where the thirteen-year-old delivered barbecue on his bicycle. At eighteen he moved into the kitchen and cooked barbecue for over five decades. In 1993 he moved around the corner to the Big S grill and added his barbecue to their soul food menu. Their wooden sign now bears his name. Hardaway represents what is called social capital. It is his knowledge that adds to the quality of life in the community

Barbecue also forms the theme of the annual SFA Symposium, an event founded in 1977 that "provides opportunities for cooks, chefs, food writers, and inquisitive eaters alike to come to a better understanding of Southern cuisine and Southern culture" (Southern Foodways Alliance 2003e).

The theme of the 2002 SFA Symposium was "Barbecue: Smoke, Sauce and History" (Southern Foodways Alliance 2003a). The event included a short film entitled *Smokestack Lightning: A Day in the Life of Barbecue,* live entertainment at the Taylor Grocery, author readings, a catfish dinner, and an event called "battling barbecue sandwiches." The closing ceremony was highlighted by a pie breakfast.

Timothy Davis, a journalist for *Gastronomica,* reported on his experiences at the Symposium (2003). He described the kickoff event, "Aberrant Barbecue Supper," which included shrimp in a butter barbecue sauce, barbecued Cornish game hens, and smoked and fried ribs. He also related his experience at the Taylor Grocery, famous for its fried catfish. Much of his article, however, consisted of barbs directed at New York-based writers and others who trivialized the event.

Georgia Gilmore

The Power of One Good Cook

I will always remember my delight when Mrs. Georgia
Gilmore—an unlettered woman of unusual intelligence—told
how an operator demanded that she got off the bus after
paying her fare and board it again by the back door, and
then drove away before she could get there. She turned to
Judge Carter and said: "When they count the money, they
do not know Negro money from white money."
—Martin Luther King Jr., March 1956

Among those individuals who have led social protest movements in
the United States such as the civil rights movement, Martin Luther
King Jr. and Rev. Jesse Jackson come to mind. However, we rarely
stop to consider the unassuming people who are not celebrities.

Mrs. Georgia Gilmore worked as a cook in a diner in Montgomery, Alabama, during the fifties. According to John T. Edge (National Public Radio 2001), Gilmore became involved with the bus
boycotts beginning in December 1955. She packed and sold chicken
sandwiches to volunteers and organized a group of women calling
themselves the Club from Nowhere who baked and sold pies and
cakes to provide money for the boycott. The name is reminiscent of
Ulysses, who called himself No Man in order to protect himself from
the cyclops Polyphemus, here being Jim Crow. Thus, when asked
who provided money to support the boycott, they could respond
truthfully "from nowhere." This also enabled white citizens to "dis-
creetly channel contributions through her" (Shriver 2000). The success of Gilmore and her friends inspired similar activities within the
community (Montgomery Bus Boycott 2004).

Gilmore was summoned to testify regarding the boycott, where
she delivered an impassioned response: "I tried to enter the front
door and the driver said, 'Nigger, give me that money.' He then told
me to get off and enter the back door. While I walked to the back
door, he drove off and left me. I decided then and there never to
ride a bus again" (Montgomery Bus Boycott 2004). This testimony

brought Gilmore into the national spotlight. As a result, she subsequently lost her job.

Despite this setback, she opened her home and fed members of the civil rights movement. Luminaries such as Martin Luther King Jr., Lyndon Baines Johnson, and Robert Kennedy ate at her table. Even though she had cooked hundreds of meals for civil rights workers (Shriver 2000), Gilmore insisted that she just served the food and let others talk (National Public Radio 2001).

Georgia Gilmore died exactly twenty-five years after the Selma-to-Montgomery march. On that day she had planned to serve fried chicken and potato salad to commemorate the anniversary (National Public Radio 2001). Like the anonymous cooks who prepare meals for their families or the line cooks who "get the food out the door" for armies of impatient customers, Gilmore's life testifies to the contribution of those unsung heroes who have enriched our culture.

A far more interesting account of the Symposium was provided by Jenel Few of the *Florida Times-Union* (2002), who interviewed Diaon Woods, a student enrolled in a hospitality program, who described her experiences from a more gustatory perspective. While she did learn about the importance of barbecue as a facet of Southern culture, Woods also encountered people whose taste knowledge of barbecue was profound. For example, they could tell what type of wood had been used to cook meat or ingredients in a sauce through just the taste. She also met people who were willing to argue passionately about their barbecue and the side dishes that accompany it. In his review R. W. Apple Jr. (2002) summarized the passion associated with what he described as "age-old questions" on the subject of barbecue: "Wood or charcoal? Pork or beef (or mutton or goat)? Chopped or sliced? Sauce based on tomatoes, vinegar or mustard? Sauce on top, sauce on the side or no sauce at all?"(A2).

As part of the Symposium, seven pit masters presented their recipes (Croom 2002). Ed Mitchell from Wilson, North Carolina, was selected to represent his state. Another component of the Symposium involved presentations by writers who have contributed to the subject of barbecue. Instead of simply describing ways to prepare barbeque, they focused on issues of race and culture.

For example, "A Confederacy of Sauces: Race Relations and the Bessinger Brothers of South Carolina" (Hitt 2002) deals with the controversy surrounding the decision of one of the Bessinger brothers to fly the Confederate flag over his barbecue joints in South Carolina to protest the state's decision to remove the controversial symbol from its capitol building. The story behind the brothers' conflict has been told many times. It reveals how strong economic and social forces can surround a phenomenon such as barbecue. These issues include the origins of barbecue in the foods of slaves, who were given scraps and leftovers for their meals (Croom 2002).

Another issue concerns who prepares food, who consumes it, as well as who eats with whom. This latter factor was part of the Bessinger brothers' conflict, since Maurice Bessinger's early restaurant allowed white patrons to park their cars under a central tin roof, while blacks were instructed to park their cars back by the wall (Hitt 2002). When Bessinger's politics were revealed in a newspaper editorial, a boycott of his restaurants and products ensued. Major retailers such as Sam's Club and Wal-Mart pulled his sauces from their shelves, resulting in his bottling plant becoming nonoperational.

It is, in part, the passion and controversy of an event such as the SFA Symposium that both attracts public attention and fosters change through education. Other symposia have included such themes as "Farm to Table" (2001) and "Appalachia" (2003). The 2004 Symposium focused on race relations. In each of these events one critical issue repeatedly surfaced: food and eating are not politically neutral. If we are to understand a specific culture, such as the American South, it is of paramount importance to know the types of food its people eat, how it is prepared, and the ways in which it is consumed.

The esssay about the Bessinger brothers' conflicts was published in *Cornbread Nation 1: The Best of Southern Food Writing* (Egerton

2002), which was supported by SFA. *Cornbread Nation 2: The United States of Barbecue* (Elie 2004) appeared more recently. These publications bring the work of many different writers to public attention while at the same time illustrating the rich interplay between food and culture in the American South.

In addition to its involvement in the Cornbread Nation series, SFA has aided in the compilation of reviews of kitchen books that reveal the role of Southern food in regional culture. One such is *Spoonbread and Strawberry Wine: Recipes and Reminiscences of a Family* by Norma Jean and Carole Darden (1994). These sisters describe several generations of their family and discuss the foods that gave them a sense of place and identity.

A third important initiative has been the annual SFA Field Trip, which was initiated in 2000. The fourth annual trip occurred in Birmingham, Alabama, and was called *"Alabama in Black and White"*. While participants celebrated the fortieth anniversary of the 1964 civil rights act, they "feasted on a Lazy Susan Supper of barbecue and biscuits and greens and sipped wines from South Africa, curated by the Palm Wine Society" (Southern Foodways Alliance 2000–3). Other field trips have included "A Taste of the Carolina Piedmont" (2001), "A Taste of Texas Barbecue" (2002) and "A Taste of Appalachia" (2003). In 2005, participants in the SFA Field Trip traveled to New Orleans to visit a new museum on Southern foods and spend time at a sugarcane plantation.

The trip to New Orleans ended just hours before the arrival of Hurricane Dennis and several months before Hurricane Katrina. In the aftermath of the Katrina disaster, the SFA immediately acted as a clearinghouse for information about members who lived in affected areas. Most recently, this organization planned a series of three-day weekends in conjunction with the Heritage Conservation Network, a nonprofit group that organizes hands-on architectural conservation workshops around the world. It's mission was to save Willie Mae's Scotch House—a landmark neighborhood restaurant in an historic vernacular building (Southern Foodways Alliance 2005).

Coincidentally, it was during the 2005 SFA Field Trip to New Orleans that the SFA recognized eighty-nine-year-old proprietor and fried chicken wizard Willie Mae Seaton with the Guardian of the Tradition award (Southern Foodways Alliance 2005).

SFA has also been involved in a variety of featured projects, such as Georgia's Lamb Barbecue, San Antonio Soul, and New Orleans Grocery. Jeff Siegel (2004) has written an interesting article about the independent grocery stores of New Orleans and their special culture. The theme of this article reflects an important aspect of the work accomplished by organizations such as SFA and Slow Food, as well as writers such as John T. Edge, in revitalizing our appreciation of regional differences worldwide.

The 2001 field trip to Piedmont SFA demonstrated one way in which the various elements of Southern food culture could be appreciated. Members visited a number of local food producers and participated in discussions about the foodways of Piedmont. However, the trip would not have been complete without the experience of enjoying great food. "A weekend of great eating begins with a beaten biscuit, country ham, and champagne tasting" (Southern Foodways Alliance, 2000–3). In another region also called Piedmont (Piedmonte in Italian), Slow Food has engaged in similar activities. Although the Salone del Gusto concluded in October 2004, there is always a good meal in the works. I am anticipating my return to both Piedmonte and Oxford—especially the Taylor Grocery and Restaurant.

References

Apple, R. W. J. 2002. "Reporter's Notebook: Age-Old Culinary Questions Still Stir a Fire." *New York Times* October 23.

Baker-Clark, C. 2001. "Great Cooks as Adult Learners: The Lore and Lure of the Kitchen." Ph.D diss.: Michigan State University.

Croom, G. 2002. "Ed Mitchell Now State's Barbecue Pitmaster." *Wilson* [N.C.] *Daily Times* October 12.

Culinary Historians of Chicago. 2001. "Grits and Greens Highlights." Accessed on December 17, 2004, at http://www.culinaryhistorians.org/news/gnghigh.htm.

Darden, N. J., and C. Darden. 1994. *Spoonbread and Strawberry Wine: Recipes and Reminiscences of a Family.* New York: Doubleday.

Davis, T. 2003. "Pigging Out." *Gastronomica* 3 (2): 11.

"Daybreak of Freedom: The Montgomery Bus Boycott." 2004. Accessed on December 17, at http://www.uncpress.unc.edu/chapters/burns_daybreak.html.

Edge, J. 1999. *A Gracious Plenty: Recipes and Recollections from the American South.* New York: G. P. Putnam's Sons.

————. 2000. *Southern Belly: The Ultimate Food Lover's Companion to the South.* Athens, Ga.: Hill Street Press.

————. 2001. *Georgia.* Oakland, Calif.: Compass American Guides.

————. 2001. "Memphis Specializes in Mutant Barbecue." *Anything Southern.* Accessed December 8, 2004, at http://www.anythingsouthern.com/articles/edge BBQspaghetti.asp.

————. 2003. Personal interview with author. July 6.

————. 2004a. *Apple Pie: An American Story.* New York: G. P. Putnam's Sons.

————. 2004b. *Fried Chicken: An American Story.* New York: G. P. Putnam's Sons.

————. 2004c. "Open House." Accessed December 17, 2004, at http://www.johntedge.com/magazines/blanche.php.

Egerton, J., ed. 2002. *Cornbread Nation 1: The Best of Southern Food Writing.* Chapel Hill:University of North Carolina Press.

Elie, L. E., ed. 2004. *Cornbread Nation 2: The United States of Barbecue.* Chapel Hill: University of North Carolina Press.

Few, J. 2002. "Future Chef Studying at GSU Learns Barbecue More Than Backyard Event." [Jacksonville] *Florida Times-Union* November 15.

Hess, K. 1998. *The Carolina Rice Kitchen: The African Connection.* Columbia: University of South Carolina Press.

Hitt, J. 2002. "A Confederacy of Sauces: Race Relations and the Bessinger Brothers of South Carolina." In *Cornbread Nation 1: The Best of Southern Food Writing,* ed. J. Egerton. Chapel Hill: University of North Carolina Press.

"Montgomery Bus Boycott: Who Was Involved?" 2004. Accessed December 17, 2004, at http://www.ajhslibrary.org/montgomery_bus_boycott%20 people.htm.

National Public Radio, 2001. "Commentary: Food and Race Issues Were

Often Intertwined in the Early Civil Rights Movement." *All Things Considered.* Accessed November 29, 2004, at http://ezproxy.gvsu. edu:2077/libweb/elib/do/document?set=search&groupid=1&requestid =lib_standard&resultid=3&edition=&ts=571CF683DB199E2B40608 A355E0F99D3_1101761167531&urn=urn%3Abigchalk%3AUS%3BB CLib%3Bdocument%3B43112715.

Shriver, J. 2000. Southern History as Told Through Its Cuisine. *USA Today* July 28.

Siegel, J. 2004. "Grocery Shopping in the Big Easy." Accessed December 18, 2004, at http://www.sothernfoodways.com/fea_nogroceries.shtml.

Southern Foodways Alliance. 2000–2003. "About the Southern Foodways Alliance." Accessed December 4, 2004, at http://www.southernfood-ways.com/about.shtml.

———. 2003a. "Barbecue: Smoke, Sauce and History." Accessed December 5, 2004, at http://www.southernfoodways.com/index.shtml.

———. 2003b. "BBQ Oral History Project." *SFA Oral History Initiative.* Accessed on December 5, 2004, at http://www.southernfoodways.com/ oral_history/tnbbq/index.shtml.

———. 2003c. "Memphis Barbecue." *SFA Oral History Initiative.* Accessed on December 5, 2004, at http://www.southernfoodways.com/ oral_history/tnbbq/moo_index.shtml.

———. 2003d. "Gathering the Stories behind the Food." *SFA Oral History Initiative.* Accessed on December 5, 2004, at http://www.southernfood-ways.com/prj_index.shtml.

———. 2003e. "Barbecue: Smoke, Sauce, and History." Southern Foodways Symposium 2002. Accessed on December 29, 2005, at http://www. southernfoodways.com/sum_02.shtml.

———. 2005. "Volunteer Vacation in New Orleans: Save Willie Mae's Scotch House." November 30. Accessed on December 29, 2005, at http://www.southernfoodways.com/index.shtml.

Voski Avakian, A., Ed. 1997. *Through the Kitchen Window: Women Explore the Intimate Meaning of Food and Cooking.* Boston: Beacon Press.

The Rediscovery of Ourselves and Food

The relationship between commitment and doubt is by
no means an antagonistic one. Commitment is healthiest
when it is not without doubt but in spite of doubt.
— Rollo May, *Love and Will*

WE LIVE IN A CULTURE in which the pace of living seems to
accelerate on a daily basis. As we are pressured to move faster and to
assume increasing responsibility, it is difficult even to consider establishing closer ties with food and food preparation. The individuals
described in this book challenge us to make such a commitment, to
dare to do so in spite of our doubts regarding the possible outcome.

Among the many lessons to be drawn from the collective experience presented here is the importance of developing an appreciation for good cooks and the craft of cooking. As Clifford Wright has
stated in his book on Mediterranean cuisine and culture, in order
for a cuisine to exist, in addition to good cooks there must also be
those who appreciate their efforts. In noting the accomplishments
of a good cook, we develop both an awareness of the culinary skills
involved as well as what constitutes quality in food preparation.

An appreciation of good cooking and good cooks, moreover, ex-
pands our knowledge of such things as taste memory, which has
played an important role in the professional lives of such great cooks

as James Beard and Julia Child. This knowledge need not be eso-teric, nor is it limited to refined palates. A case in point is provided by Mark Schaub, an educator who is neither a cook nor a self-pro-claimed gourmet, who developed an appreciation for barbecue joints, especially those that offer barbecued beef brisket. He does not care too much for "chain barbecue restaurants," but when he and his family visit Texas and other regions where brisket is popular, he usually asks local residents to recommend a place, such as a neighbor-hood independent diner. Schaub has thus transformed eating brisket into a craft and is eager to share his knowledge with others.

In contemporary American culture it has become difficult to develop such an appreciation because we are surrounded by mass production and distribution of foods. Upon closer scrutiny, even items designated "gourmet" or homemade are no more than manu-factured foods that have been appealingly packaged to give the ap-pearance of superior quality.

One could rightly argue that cooking in the United States has experienced a renaissance, as evidenced by the proliferation of food-related broadcasts on television and an explosion of cookbooks, as well as autobiographies by celebrity chefs. However, this boom has also inspired the term "food voyeur." Those "trophy kitchens" in the homes of the affluent are mere staging areas for reheating foods picked up in supermarket delis on the way home from work. These cultural artifacts seem to have bypassed people like Velma Hutch-ings, Mildred Council, and Georgia Gilmore. Do we not owe some respect to those unseen—and often unrewarded—individuals who prepare meals as part of their daily routine?

It is from the lives of these great cooks that we learn much about the craft of cooking. The acquisition of this craft, however, demands dedication and hard work and cannot be accomplished through technology or the amassing of cookbooks. Learning in the kitch-en is a lifelong process. Nowhere is this more evident than in the careers of great cooks such as Susan Spicer, whose knowledge was acquired through sweat and tears. The lives of these individuals suggest that the acquisition and practice of the craft of cooking is just as important as its end product—good food. The journey is just as valuable—and enjoyable—as the destination. Trial and error is an integral part of this process. A growing mastery of the fonds, or fundamentals, inspires a sense of self-reliance and engenders creativity in the kitchen, where, for example, stale bread becomes part of a stuffing and leftover green beans are recycled to produce a pot of fresh vegetable soup.

Despite the fact that mastering the art of cooking demands concentration and an investment of time, the knowledge needed to do so is not arcane. This is well-illustrated by John Bartlett in his wonderful cookbook *The Peasant Gourmet*, who writes that "those sumptuous repasts that have for so long regaled the gourmet have their origins in the solid fare served at the peasant's table, in his improvisations, his celebrations, and his ability to make do with nature in her bounty, or lack of it, bestowed on him" (ix).

Another important lesson is to become more adventuresome in one's eating and cooking. This is reflected in the lives of Julia and Paul Child, who explored the cuisines of India and China; in the comments of Mark Schaub, who can't wait to try a diner known for its great breakfasts and a cook who refuses to prepare eggs "sunny side down"; and in the emotional recollections of John T. Edge, who reflects on the many gastronomic adventures he undertook in the company of his father.

Cooking can also be learned by spending time with people who enjoy preparing good food, which also results in lasting social friendships. This was a powerful source of learning for Julia Child.

People who share a common interest in good food know where to obtain quality ingredients. Small markets that cater to such clients are great places to educate one's palate. A case in point is Frank's Market in Grand Rapids, Michigan. Located on Market Street, on the west side of Grand Rapids, the market has become a fixture in the community. Owned and operated by the same family for three generations, here you can purchase homemade sausages and custom-trimmed meats. You can gossip about food with other patrons or learn a new way to prepare that well-marbled cut of meat you just purchased.

People who enjoy good food can also be found at farmers' markets. Some of these markets house large numbers of vendors and are interesting places to explore. Locally produced cured meats and cheeses made from raw milk are just two of the many items you might find. Farmers' markets have become gathering places, providing public spaces where people can connect and develop a sense of community.

Perhaps the most important contribution of farmers' markets is that they place people in closer proximity to the land and the people who produce our food. These markets also foster an appreciation of local and regional foods. Like M. F. K. Fisher and James Beard, we can seek out locally produced varieties of apples or artisanal cheeses and fresh-churned butter.

It is in these common spaces that knowledge as well as commodities can be exchanged. Here we can discover new ingredients or techniques. What is the best way to store fresh tomatoes? When will the peaches show up at the market? All too often this knowledge is not readily available in superstores, where clerks are pressured to fill display cases and shelves as rapidly as possible. For example, the clerk in the meat department of one of these stores probably does not even know the grades of beef specified by the Department of Agriculture.

An important way in which Julia Child, James Beard, and others like them continued to learn the craft of cooking was by teaching the craft to others, which became an important component of their lives. Their lessons, moreover, were not limited to technical matters. They discussed the excitement of learning about foods from foreign cultures, the importance of sharing food with others, and the unmitigated satisfaction associated with simple, well-prepared foods. Thus, teaching and learning the craft of cookery in both formal and informal contexts can prove extremely rewarding.

A special form of teaching and learning about food involves parents and children who prepare meals together. This process should not be perceived as simply an efficient way to perform routine chores. Even the preparation of a grilled cheese sandwich can become an adventure.

Another way in which children can become involved in the food-preparation process is by visiting local farms where individuals pick their own produce. Harvesting local produce also helps us to better appreciate the importance of seasonal foods. Engaging children in food preparation can be a daunting task, since many parents do not possess the basic cooking skills themselves. In these circumstances it is all too easy to fall back on a bread machine or packaged mixes. While these gadgets are good entry points into the world of cooking, it is far more rewarding to follow the advice of such individuals as Father Dominic, who encourages people to use their hands when working with dough. Mixing and kneading dough are activities that can be performed with little or no skill. Making bread also provides us with an opportunity to slow down and enjoy each other's company while munching a fresh slice of bread spread with butter or homemade preserves. By simply mixing ingredients for bread in a bowl and kneading the dough by hand, we also become more closely connected with our food.

The process of making and eating bread engages our senses. It may involve repeated attempts and will invariably include mistakes. This is the heart of the learning process, and it should be pleasurable. The creation of simple foods by parents and children can provide both with a sense of accomplishment. This feeling of mastery can lead to other culinary adventures. Food-related events at the community level create lasting traditions that foster a sense of identity for those involved. Morris, Illinois, holds an annual corn festival and Henderson, Kentucky, sponsors its annual W. C. Handy Blues & Barbecue Festival. Many of these food festivals have been around for generations, helping to promote a sense of regional identity. For example, people from the Upper Peninsula in Michigan have the pasty (a turnover made from a folded-over round of pastry with a filling in the middle), while Texans can brag about their ancestors' role in the creation of chili. The Chili Appreciation Society International (CASI) uses its events to promote chili, encourage camaraderie, and to raise funds for nonprofit organizations as well as a scholarship program.

Families also carry on food traditions that are not limited to the annual Thanksgiving Day turkey or hot dogs on the Fourth of July. They often hand down special recipes from one generation to the next and hold events that involve food. Traditions such as these help preserve family identities and even ethnic heritages, which today are at risk of being lost as a result of media blitzes promoting fast food over more traditional ethnic foods.

Whether you attend a family reunion, a community-wide food celebration, or a neighborhood chili cook-off, there is always an opportunity to taste new foods and to learn about how they are prepared. Even those of us who live in areas where there are no obvious food traditions associated with local culture or who lack extended families can still create our own food identities—perhaps the greatest challenge facing us in today's gastronomic culture.

Reference

Bartlett, J. 1975. *The Peasant Gourmet.* New York: Macmillan.

Index